Milton Babbitt *Words About Music*

Milton Babbitt *Words About Music*

Edited by Stephen Dembski and Joseph N. Straus

THE MADISON LECTURES

The University of Wisconsin Press

Published 1987

The University of Wisconsin Press
114 North Murray Street
Madison, Wisconsin 53715

The University of Wisconsin Press, Ltd.
1 Gower Street
London WC1E 6HA, England

First printing

Printed in the United States of America

For LC CIP information see the colophon

ISBN 0-299-10790-6

The following publishers have generously given permission to use material from copyrighted works:
Examples 1-16, 1-17, 1-18 from *String Quartet no. 2* by Milton Babbitt, copyright 1967 by Associated
Music Publishers Inc.; and examples 3-1, 3-2, 3-8, 3-9 from *Quartet no. 4* by Arnold Schoenberg,
copyright 1967 by Associated Music Publishers Inc. Used by special arrangement with G. Shirmer Inc.
Example 3-10 from *Klavierstücke* by Arnold Schoenberg, op. 33a, mm. 1-2, copyright 1929 by
Universal, copyright renewed 1956 by Gertrude Schoenberg; and examples 3-12, 3-17 from *Moses und
Aron* by Arnold Schoenberg (orchestral score) mm. 1–7 and three measures at Moses' entrance,
copyright 1977 by B. Schott's Söhne. Used by permission of Belmont Music Publishers, Los Angeles,
California 90049.
Example 5-25 from *Five Pieces for Orchestra* by Arnold Schoenberg, op. 16, first movement, mm. 1–
5 (orchestral score), copyright 1952 by Henmar Press Inc. Example 5-26 from the Webern reduction
for two pianos of the same Schoenberg work, copyright 1913 by C. F. Peters, Leipzig. Used by permission of C. F. Peters Corporation, New York.

Contents

Chapter Five/Professional Theorists and Their Influence 121

Professional theorists . . . The Schenker synthesis and a Bach chorale . . . Erpf and the emergence of the contextual point of view . . . Schenker's analysis of a Bach chorale and some additional parallelisms . . . Diminution technique . . . A contextual analysis of the Prelude to *Tristan* . . . Eccentric but influential theorists . . . Erpf's *Kette*, *Klirrtöne*, etc. . . . Contextual continuity techniques in Hindemith's Third String Quartet and Schoenberg's *Five Pieces for Orchestra*, Opus 16 and *Klavierstücke*, Opus 23 No. 3.

Chapter 6/The Unlikely Survival of Serious Music 163

The intellectual and social reorientation of music in this century as a result of compositional contextuality . . . Schoenberg's search for communality . . . Electronic music and the human ear as the new source of boundary conditions . . . Words about music . . . The composer in academia and the attitude of his fellow academics towards composition . . . The special problems of the American composer.

Preface

In the fall of 1983, Milton Babbitt spent two weeks at the School of Music of the University of Wisconsin at Madison, giving lectures and leading seminars on a variety of subjects. Although Babbitt is best known as a composer, he has also produced an extraordinary body of theoretical work. The emergence in the past forty years of professional music theory (traced by Babbitt in Chapter 5) is, to a significant degree, Babbitt's own doing. His theoretical efforts, like his compositional efforts, have been primarily in the area of twelve-tone music. Virtually all theoretical and analytical work of significance in this area has built on the foundation he established. But his influence in theoretical matters has spread far beyond this single area. Though less widely known, his analytical insights regarding tonal music, of which Chapter 5 provides a sampling, have had a profound effect on sophisticated work in that domain, bringing to bear on it conceptual tools first developed for twelve-tone theory. And his concern with "words about music," and with what he calls "verbal and methodological responsibility," have set the standard for theoretical inquiry throughout the discipline. It is no exaggeration to call him the founding father of professional music theory. But apart from his students, and those who have penetrated the dense prose of his articles in professional music-theoretical journals, few have had direct exposure to his ideas about music.

During his time at Madison, Babbitt spoke on many topics which have been central to his teaching at Princeton and Juilliard for the past forty years. He spoke to a variety of audiences, from a specially constituted graduate seminar focused on his music and associated theoretical issues to an unrestricted group of musicians and nonmusicians; therefore, he approached these topics from many different points of view. Altogether, these lectures presented a concise summary of many of his most essential theoretical insights, but because of the pedagogical context, the language is informal and explanatory.

When the tape recordings that had been made were transcribed, we found ourselves with a mass of unique material. As we began to prepare it for publication, we were pulled in two opposing directions. First, we wished to preserve the dazzling constructions and spontaneous excitement of Babbitt's spoken language. He is, as he says, "somewhat known as a talker," and we wanted in no way to compromise the inimitable personal quality of his speech. At the same time, any spoken language contains elements which need modification to work well on the printed page. It was thus clear that some degree of editing would be necessary.

Our editorial work involved primarily cutting extraneous material, supplying punctuation, providing some transitions, and coordinating references to musical examples which Babbitt wrote at the blackboard and which we reconstructed from our notes. Occasionally, when a passage required reworking for the written format, we would work with him to develop the appropriate language. But, in general, we worked directly from the actual transcripts and used Babbitt's own language: we have tried to smooth the rough edges, but the words are his. For those who might be interested, the original tape recordings and transcripts are available at the Mills Music Library of the University of Wisconsin–Madison.

The lectures and seminars that make up this book were addressed to a variety of audiences with varying degrees of training in music theory. The first and last chapters were addressed, respectively, to a class of college sophomores studying twentieth-century music and to a general audience: these chapters assume little or no formal training in music. The fifth chapter is from a graduate seminar in the history of music theory and, while analytical, is not highly technical. The second, third, and fourth make up the theoretical core of the book, and as presentations in the specially constituted seminar referred to above, they do assume a basic knowledge of atonal and twelve-tone theory. John Rahn's *Basic Atonal Theory* (New York: Longman, 1980), one of the central textbooks in this area, provides a more than adequate background and is terminologically similar to Babbitt's own work. For quick reference, we have provided a brief glossary of the most important terms.

We have provided a few explanatory footnotes but, in general, we have decided to let Babbitt explain things in his own way. At times, he does not give full explanations of terms as they are introduced. Instead, he often prefers to develop a concept with examples, allowing the explanation to emerge from the presentation. This method of explanation corresponds to the nature of the argument throughout these lectures. At times, Babbitt's presentation seems elliptical and digressive. But however far afield the discussion seems to range, we found for ourselves that a coherent line of argument always lies beneath the surface. Almost like the basic structural material that informs his music, the central unifying argument in each of these lectures is "there in a very decisive way so that it's continuously, thoroughly, and utterly influential, but in constantly different ways and in constantly different degrees of explicitness, and acting at various distances from the surface."

Many people helped us in preparing this book. Larry Arnold, Lenore Hiebert, and Anne O'Donnell took on the difficult job of transcribing the tape recordings. Anne O'Donnell skillfully deciphered our (occasionally conflicting) editorial marks to create a clean manuscript for the publisher. Allen Fitchen of the University of Wisconsin Press was enthusiastically supportive of this publication from its inception. Tina Hafemeister, in her characteristically elegant hand, prepared autographs of the musical examples. Jeff Stadelman prepared the index. As the manuscript neared completion, Chester Biscardi, Susan Blaustein, and Martin Brody studied it carefully and suggested many clarifications. Sally Goldfarb and Paul De Angelis provided helpful assistance in other areas.

Babbitt's residency in Madison—the occasion for these lectures—was made possible by a generous grant from the William F. Vilas Estate. And finally, we would like to acknowledge our deep gratitude to Eunice Meske, Director of the School of Music at the University of Wisconsin–Madison, for her unflagging and invaluable support, from the initial idea of inviting Babbitt to Madison to this publication of his lectures. Without her enthusiasm and assistance this project would never have been conceived, much less completed.

For us, this has been a labor of love. Milton Babbitt is a singular man, and during our work on this book, we have come to know him better. We began the project with admiration and warm affection for him, feelings which have only intensified during our work together. We complete it with feelings of profound gratitude for the opportunity to have worked closely with him on this unusual expression of his thinking in and about music.

Milton Babbitt *Words About Music*

1 The Twelve-Tone Tradition

Many years ago it came to my ears that there were people out there (none composers) who intimated that there were those of us composers, at least some of us composers, who wrote our music with at least one ear directed towards its susceptibility to public exegesis. That is, we wrote our music so that we could talk about it. Now whether or not I'm one of those who was supposed to have so perversely polluted the pure act of creation, I can only say that that's not at all the way I write music but, above all, that's not the way I want to talk about music. I am somewhat known as a talker, and words about music concern me very much, but the truth of the matter is that there's nothing I find more difficult to do than talk about music and, above all, talk about my own music. This is not some kind of an academic ploy, I promise you. When you're confronted by an occasion like this (or an opportunity like this), there's the very strong temptation to justify yourself. It's very hard to justify yourself as a composer anyhow, but to justify yourself as a living American composer is even worse. There is a terrible temptation to seize such an opportunity and point with pride to the individual achievements of your works, to direct the listeners' attention to those individualities, those originalities of the pieces that you've written which somehow justify their existence. No matter how aware you may be of the fact that a prophet is celebrated after the fact historically, and mainly by his name and not by his music, there's a terrible temptation to point to the singularities of your pieces and, therefore, stake a claim as a prophet in at least your own time and place. So that's what you're likely to do.

Now the truth of the matter is that to point to the singularities, the originalities (if indeed they exist), to point to that which is (in the composer's view) historically unprecedented and chronologically unparalleled, probably does less good for the listener (who has heard very little, if any, of your music and is likely in the future to hear very little) than another approach. So, rather than putting up four notes and showing you what I've done with them, or having you listen to a piece and obliging you to agree that it's rather singular in its accomplishment, I think it would make much more sense simply to say something about the tradition from which the music derives, no matter how far beneath the surface this tradition manifests itself, and no matter how recent the tradition itself may be. That's what you're likely to do if you approach this matter with any real desire to have yourself understood— or rather, I should say, have your music understood (I'd rather be misunderstood myself than have my music misunderstood). So that is what I will do, particularly in view of the music that you have been listening to, studying, and, I trust, loving.

But there's another temptation, another danger, here. It's almost inevitable that one's going to talk about pieces of music in the context of other pieces of music. And the danger is that if you begin talking about the tradition which your music presumes to extend and from which it derives, you begin looking at a piece of music as a kind of sample, a statistical sample from a musical population. At the same time, I think most of us try as much as we possibly can to hear a piece of music, to absorb a piece of music, to understand a piece of music as a singular, individuated accomplishment. Now obviously, this is a matter of degree. You can't possibly regard a piece as totally ad hoc, and you can't possibly regard a piece of music as having nothing to do with anything but itself. On the other hand, you can't possibly regard a piece of music as being totally of a tradition and having no individual characteristics. There are pieces that come mighty close, but none can achieve it.

So this is where we start: I'm going to brave all the dangers. The first pieces that I now call my own—the first pieces I wrote when I went back to composition after many years of not being allowed to compose because there was a war—date from 1947/48. If you looked at any of those pieces (or if you were told by somebody), you'd find that they were all twelve-tone, twelve-pitch-class—whatever words you want to use—compositions, but I think that would tell you very little about my music or probably anybody else's music. That is not just a glib surface statement; it's something very deep and has a great deal to do with many of the issues that arose with contemporary music.

Back in the thirties, I began becoming interested in the music of Schoenberg. Schoenberg arrived on the shores of this country, in New York, in October 1933, a date that shall live in my memory. As good luck would have it, he was interviewed on the boat as he arrived by a man who was then working for a musical magazine and with whom I had grown up in Jackson, Mississippi (you see what a small world this is). Through this connection, I met Schoenberg when he came to this country, when I went to New York. I had come from Mississippi; he had come from Vienna, Berlin, Paris. And, though he probably had had better food, he had the same kind of culture shock that I did. The man who went to meet him at the boat was named Lehman Engel[1]— some of you who know about musical comedy may know the name. He was a very famous Broadway conductor, and he died very recently. But at that time he was a composer and was just picking up a living by interviewing people in music for a magazine called *Musical Leader*, which is long since gone.[2] He couldn't speak German, and Schoenberg, who never learned to speak English very well, spoke very little English at that time. Lehman said, "Here is a little present for you," and gave him a message from some of his colleagues in this country. Schoenberg had been, of course, totally displaced, and he was there with his little daughter and his wife. Schoenberg said, "Thank you," which he had learned to say, and Lehman said, "You're welcome," which people say in some parts of the world. And Schoenberg began to cry because he thought Lehman had meant, "You're welcome to this country." It's a very touching story.

I got to know Schoenberg then, so I want to tell you a little about the atmosphere at the time. I think some tremendous misunderstandings persist, and therefore, before I talk about my view of Schoenberg and therefore my view of me, I want to talk a little bit about these. Back in the thirties, the name of Schoenberg was already a monumental name in this country. I'm speaking entirely as someone who was a young composition student at that time. His was a great, great name, but his music was known virtually not at all—certainly not his most recent music. And the late music, such pieces as the Fourth Quartet and the Violin Concerto, hadn't been written yet, although it was just about to be written. Schoenberg at the time had already started working on his Violin Concerto and then wrote his Fourth Quartet. It's of great sociological interest that the Violin Concerto—completed here—wasn't performed until 1940 and his Fourth Quartet not until the late thirties. He was greatly disappointed by this. He was crushed by the fact that these works were not widely performed. Schoenberg, you see, was rather naive. That his works were not widely performed and widely celebrated changed him a great deal with regard to composing. It had a tremendous effect upon him. He felt that he had been a failure in this country and he tried writing works that he naively thought would be great hits—you know, on the hit parade. He did an arrangement of a Brahms chamber music work and he finished his Second Chamber Symphony. These were works that would normally be called tonal. He wrote to Fritz Reiner about one of the works—the *Variations* Opus 43 (a band piece: you see, that's American)—and he said, "This is not one of my main works because it is not a composition with twelve tones."[3]

The Europeans criticized his "American works," forgetting that at least two of his greatest works—the Fourth Quartet and the Violin Concerto—were American works. However, his reception here did have a strong effect on him and on his music. That reception included total misunderstanding of Schoenberg, even among people who had the best faith in the world and who were trying very hard to understand what he was all about. Remember, you couldn't hear the music—none of it was recorded. There was no way to hear even middle Schoenberg. No one could hear *Erwartung*, which had been done once in this country, or *Pierrot Lunaire*. The first *Pierrot Lunaire* recording was made by Schoenberg himself in this country. There were no recordings of any of this music so there was no way that you could possibly hear it.

So what did you do? You went to a place called the Fifty-eighth Street Library in New York City. You weren't allowed to take out these scores, because they were extremely expensive and very valuable. Very few people could afford to buy them. So you tried to hear them mentally. You crushed your little minds trying to hear them. The very first book that had anything to do with the whole twelve-tone idea was written by Ernst Krenek. The date was 1936. It was very obscure, published by an obscure Viennese publisher in very obscure Viennese German. A few people got hold of it and read it, but very few people even knew that it existed. Virtually nothing was known about this music, and what was known was really a very strange form of knowledge indeed.

Let me be autobiographical again. In the thirties, you could go to any university you wanted to. Harvard couldn't fill its freshman class. You just moved around from school to school very easily. Many people couldn't afford to go to college. I could afford to go to college, so when I didn't like the school, I left. I didn't like many schools. I ended up at Washington Square College of New York University for lots of reasons. It was the place to be in those days, intellectually. But there was something else. A book had just appeared called *Twentieth-Century Music* by a wonderful lady named Marion Bauer, whose name I'm going to do everything in the world to immortalize. The book has just been republished and I've written a little preface to it.[4] Marion Bauer was no analyst and she was no theorist. She was more of a composer. But she was very much concerned to do everything she could to make known contemporary music that she thought was worthwhile. Schoenberg had this book in his archive when he died because, of course, it pleaded him a great giant and spent a great deal of time on him.

So here you opened a book, and for the first time—not only in English, but in virtually any language—you had examples from Schoenberg, examples from Stravinsky, examples from everyone you could think of. And the examples from Schoenberg were not examples from *Verklaerte Nacht*. They were examples from the Opus 11 *Piano Pieces* and from *Pierrot Lunaire*. So anyone who was interested in contemporary music saw this book (they didn't care what she said, because she didn't say very much—there were many quotations from other people) and rushed to Washington Square to be with someone who cared about this music, and many did. So we found ourselves in New York in the summer of 1934, with Schoenberg living up Broadway at the Ansonia Hotel. We were all told he was going to teach at NYU the following year, and Juilliard offered him a job. It cannot be said that academic institutions were not aware of who Schoenberg was. The trouble was he was a very, very sick man, and he said he couldn't stand another New York winter. (He should be out here in Wisconsin!) He felt he had to go to California.

I tell you all this because it crucially affected the lives of those of us who got to know Schoenberg. There were people then who were aware of the importance of this man, aware at least of the striking—and in many cases the problematical—nature of his music. They simply wanted to come to terms with it and found it very difficult to do so. Schoenberg had left New York, but in the meantime he had left behind a trail. His music was beginning to be looked at—still not played—and composers three times my age took an interest in it and approached me because they knew that I was interested in this music and that I had talked to Schoenberg a little (actually I knew him only very slightly). These were skillful composers who were well known in their own domain. They would say to me, "This twelve-tone thing seems interesting. I've tried working with it but it gives me problems. I'm okay for the first seven or eight notes, but then for the last four or five notes—I don't know what to do with them." The temptation always was to say, "Well, stick them in the contrabassoon and nobody will notice!"

This kind of misapprehension however reflected a much deeper one: the notion that twelve-tone music involved counting up to twelve. There were all kinds of strictures that people imagined were associated with this (some people liked strictures; others resented them as being mechanistic). People imagined that you couldn't repeat a note until all twelve had been sounded. Well obviously such people had never looked at a piece that anybody called twelve-tone. Such a terrible confusion of the representation of a set or a series or a row with the whole conception of the structural function of ordering was pathetic and led to fundamental misunderstandings, many of which, I'm afraid, still persist.

There were other things, too, including the notion of the identification of the horizontal and the vertical. Of course Schoenberg never said that, although it's been quoted: he talked about the unity of musical space, but he meant something very special.[5] He meant the derivation of counterpoint from certain linear things, which you encounter, for example, in the Fourth Quartet. They're more obvious in the third movement than the first. Some people got the notion that he meant that whatever goes up must go sideways, or something like that. The misunderstandings were so great, and, after all, what was said about the music very much determined how people listened to it. They listened for things that weren't there, and never were there, and if they were there, they wouldn't be very interesting. The fundamental misapprehensions were so great that what was transmitted was a kind of approach to listening to this music which delighted some (because there was a kind of literalness about it that they thought they could follow) and repelled others.

For Schoenberg the twelve-tone notion was a response to something he felt very keenly, namely, a certain inadequacy in the middle music that he had written—*Erwartung, Pierrot Lunaire*—and also the pieces of Berg's middle period, such as the *Three Pieces for Orchestra*, and Webern's middle pieces like the Opus 10 *Orchestra Pieces*. Schoenberg said very explicitly that he was dissatisfied. He was a very honest man, a man desperately trying to write, in some sense, the greatest music ever. We all try to do that—most of us do, anyhow. And I think in his case it was much more explicitly a desire to be part of that great tradition. In an attempt to define his historical position, he redefined Bach as his predecessor and Brahms as a progressive. An effort to define one's relation to the great tradition is typical of Schoenberg and the other Viennese. Schoenberg was perfectly willing to be candid: he referred to his composition in those middle periods as "composing with the tones of a motive."[6] Now, you see, that already defines a high degree of self-reference and contextuality. Forgive me that term *contextuality*—you're going to be hearing much too much of it from me. But the fact is that I know no other term that's as good. To some extent, I've stolen it from other fields, which is something I like to do. I don't like to manufacture terms. I don't want to say *motivic*. *Self-referential* is also a very good term, which means that, as much as possible, you make a work self-enclosed. You define its principles—a progression of relatedness—within itself. Now again that's relative; contextuality has to be relative. When you talk about a piece and talk about the relation between a theme here and a theme there or how something is transformed or how something relates, you're talking about contextual characteristics, characteristics internal to the particular piece. This is a matter of degree—and matters of degree can be crucial where musical intelligibility is concerned.

For an example of "composing with the tones of a motive," there is a five-note motive which gave rise to Opus 23, Number 3, which in many ways is still one of the most complex pieces that Schoenberg ever wrote. It's not a twelve-tone piece, obviously. I said obviously merely because of the opus number, not because of the five-note motive at the beginning. From that moment forth, those five notes as a succession, as a collection, are going to be interpreted and reinterpreted to provide the criteria for counterpoint and harmony.

The problem is perfectly obvious. Suppose you're confronted by a tape of someone speaking a language to which you have no relation whatsoever. It belongs to a language family that has no relation to any language you know at all. Because you are listening to a tape, you don't see the person speaking, you don't see any gestures, you don't see anything that might amplify any kind of semantic basis. How much of a sample do you think you would need before you would even know where there are word divisions, or articulations? Would the best technique for someone trying to teach you the language that way be to take very small segments and slightly modify them, or to give you a long sample? This is basically the problem.

Now I'm not making linguistic analogies at all; those are extremely hazardous. But there is a certain basis at least for some sort of heuristic understanding of what Schoenberg regarded as the problem. The problem was that you were basically having to deal with rather small-scale ideas: you had to do things rather literally and you were carrying the hearer along. Then there was a much larger problem. When the listener went from this piece to another similarly constructed piece, he could carry very little of the experience of that last piece to the next piece. In other words, Schoenberg was seeking, believe it or not, a new communality—he said as much.

He thought he had his new communality with the twelve-tone idea. When you write a piece, of this composing-with-the-tones-of-a-motive sort, it's quite obvious that all you will have in common from that piece to the next piece may be some devices of composing. You notice that "composing with the tones of a motive" seems to suggest a pitch-oriented conception, and indeed it was.

Schoenberg began his career in Vienna and taught private students there. They included the celebrated ones, Berg and Webern, and some less celebrated ones—I won't bore you with the names—but in all they were a remarkable group. Then he went to Berlin, where he taught the master composition class at the Prussian Academy, of all places. He had a remarkable group of students around him then, too. They've been forgotten, although the fault is not theirs: most of them were wiped out. There was, for example, a man named Norbert Von Hannenheim, whom Ernst Krenek, Stravinsky, and many other composers considered the greatest genius of his generation. Norbert Von Hannenheim, in spite of the name, was a Romanian who studied with Schoenberg in Berlin.[7] He, and all of his music, disappeared. So that's what happened to the Berlin circle.

An American of German background, Adolph Weiss, wrote an article called "The Lyceum of Schoenberg" reporting in a very matter-of-fact and very limited manner the things that Schoenberg taught people to do with the motive.[8] This was a composition seminar, but it wasn't the nice kind of loose thing we Americans do these days. Instead, Schoenberg would tell you how to compose. What he taught were not sufficient conditions; they were necessary conditions; and I hope that distinction is clear. He wasn't saying that if you do this, you will therefore create great or coherent or marvelous music. But he was saying that if you don't do this, your music will be worthless. It's a different stake. They dealt in absolutes that many of us cannot deal in because of a different kind of educational background.

But Schoenberg began to feel dissatisfied with such absolutes, and he began to formulate the twelve-tone notion—and I remind you of how many years it took, how many false starts it took. He began writing in the teens a work called *Jakobsleiter* (*Jacob's Ladder*). He wrote about 450–500 measures of that piece—I say "about" because he left it unfinished. Although it is unfinished, it already almost runs longer than my collected lifework. And despite being unfinished, it's an extraordinary piece; remember, *Moses and Aaron* is unfinished too. But this extraordinary piece begins with six pitches unaccompanied in the bass and two three-note chords in woodwinds, ordered as in example 1-1; then it goes on, "composing with the tones of the motive."

EXAMPLE 1-1

Now that looks like a twelve-tone series, or row, or set. I generally use the word *set;* let me explain why. When Schoenberg came to this country, he knew very little English, as I've already said. There were two words for "row" or "series" or "set" in German. One of them was *Reihe,* for which there is no obvious translation. The other was *Folge,* which very few people realized was constantly being used in the literature of that time. Native speakers of German would call it a "succession." When Schoenberg came to this country, he realized that everybody had taken *Reihe* and translated it literally as "row." Well, Schoenberg was a very serious man, sometimes perhaps a bit solemn about his seriousness. He saw this expression being translated as "row," and he went to his dictionary; he came up with some wonderful things. (Try going to a dictionary sometimes and speaking the language from it! His English simply never became idiomatic at all, although he insisted upon speaking English. He always spoke English to me, though I understand German. He insisted upon it, because he felt it would be insulting if he couldn't speak your native language. He would also be insulted if you tried to speak German back to him. He thought he had to learn English, and one honored this, of course.) The word *Reihe* bothered him because it became *row.* And to him *row* suggested left to right—something in a row—and that's what it does connote. And that connotation, he thought, was part of all these misunderstandings about the twelve-tone notion having to do with some sort of thematic, motivic thing that went from left to right. It upset him, so he asked various friends about it.

Now the word that I preferred and still prefer is the word *series.* The word *series* is a very decent one, because all it involves is a very special relation that has been defined for centuries as a term of abstract relation theory: seriation. It applies to a succession of notes ordered in any way that you can perceive them in music: for example, in time and space and by dynamics. It's simply a series relationship. It's irreflexive, it's asymmetric, and it's transitive; and that's exactly what it is, so, therefore, the reasonable thing is to use the word that everybody's been using in civilized society for about a hundred years and call it *series*. But Schoenberg had German friends, and German friends always know English better than we natives. So they said, "Oh no, you can't use the word *series*, because *series* always implies a plus or a minus as in 'an arithmetical series' or 'a geometrical series' or 'a trigonometric series.'" This is nonsense, of course. But they were mathematicians, so he said, "No, I can't use *series*."

And I regret to tell you, I am guilty. I suggested the word *set*, which had absolutely no meaning in music as yet. It came out of mathematics (not that that pleased me particularly) and it seemed to be a neutral term. Of course, a set does not mean anything ordered, but if you append *twelve-tone* or *twelve-pitch-class* to the word *set*, then that implies an ordered set and that's a very familiar structure, too, in abstract relation theory. So there we were. The trouble was that having been given the word *set* (and he was delighted with it), Schoenberg went out to California and, of course, immediately became corrupted. Somebody gave him the term *basic set*, which he then used very often, as if there were some a priori basic set. This can induce as much confusion as anything else. For example, consider the following: If somebody said of our example 1-1, "Is that a twelve-tone set?" the answer is, "How can I possibly tell?" If I go to the piano and, in my own inimitable style, play example 1-2 and say, "Is this a tonic triad?" what would your response be?

EXAMPLE 1-2

How can you possibly know? You can't conceivably know because it's a contextual, dispositional thing. First of all, you're not even sure it's a triad. It may be a dissonance. It may be G–C♭–D. People forget that consonance and dissonance are not absolutes; they're purely contextual.

You have no way of knowing that I'm playing a consonance when I play the following:

EXAMPLE 1-3

I insist I'm playing C–F♭. It could very well be C–F♭, but C–F♭, by definition of any tonal literature that I know, is a dissonance. So even consonance and dissonance are matters of context. But let's assume the context is established and that example 1-2 is a G-major triad. The crucial point is that you have no way of knowing that it's a *tonic* triad. We have all the standard examples to illustrate this point: we have the one about the First Symphony of Beethoven being in F; we have the one about the First Ballade of Chopin being in A♭. There are many instances where the first triad turns out contextually not to be the centric, tonic triad.

By the same token, to say that example 1-1 is a twelve-tone set is ridiculous. It becomes so only by centric function, by dispositional function, by its function, its use in the piece. It is not a twelve-tone set, because *Jakobsleiter* is not a twelve-tone piece. Rather, in it Schoenberg was "composing with the tones of a motive." There are all kinds of remarkable psychological as well as musical consequences of this. In 1944 Schoenberg went back to this piece, and he couldn't finish it, because by then he was thinking totally differently about music. So he said, "Look, I have twelve different pitch classes identified registrally at the beginning of this piece. I can turn this into a twelve-tone piece." He began working with it, but, after only about forty-four or forty-five measures of it, he couldn't continue. Nobody knows why he couldn't continue and complete the piece. He started it again with the idea of writing a twelve-tone piece and apparently couldn't cope with this kind of hexachord. He couldn't combine the hexachord with an inversional form of itself to get an aggregate, and that seemed to have stopped him in his tracks. He could have gotten aggregates, of course, by retrograde-inversional forms, but he didn't seem to be aware of it. He really didn't know what to do with those hexachords when he went back to rewrite the piece.

He had written a huge piece and left it unfinished. At that stage of his life, the idea of writing the whole thing over again from a twelve-tone point of view—and then finishing it—probably exhausted him, and he was not able to cope with it. That was toward the end of his composing career, and he was terribly blind. That may have had more to do with it than anything else. Of course, he never expected anyone to perform *Jakobsleiter* in its unfinished state.

There are other pieces by Schoenberg which use self-inversional hexachords, but none of these are *just* self-inversional. Schoenberg never understood the generality of the principles involved. The sketches for the Piano Concerto, for example, show him starting over and over again, trying to find the inversional hexachords. Toward the end of his life, he wrote the *Modern Psalms,* a set of little pieces for which he wrote the text. He never realized that the series he used there—a third-order all-combinatorial series—he had already used in the *Ode to Napoleon* and in the Opus 29 Suite. He didn't realize it was exactly the same hexachord. He never thought of these hexachords except in a particular ordering, and he never saw the generality of the unordered form, at least not until he got to the *Violin Fantasy,* where he basically just works with the hexachords individually. So he didn't realize that way back in Opus 29 he had already used a series which was both inversionally combinatorial and also self-inversional. When he returned to the *Jakobsleiter* hexachords, which are only self-inversional, he gave up. For him, the way to begin a piece was to find a pair of hexachords which not only would combine to form an aggregate but were also inversionally related. The *Jakobsleiter* hexachords were not.

The reason he couldn't continue is thus a fundamentally, profoundly technical one having to do with the structure of the hexachords.

EXAMPLE 1-4

Compare them (ex. 1-4) to those of Schoenberg's Fourth Quartet, for example, each of which is the collectional inversion of its complement (see ex. 1-7), like most of Schoenberg's hexachords. The *Jakobsleiter* hexachords are also combinatorial, but in a different way: they are the collectional inversions of themselves—they are self-inversional.[9]

Still, the *Jakobsleiter* hexachords are combinatorial; Schoenberg was intuitively thinking ahead to twelve-tone things. I use the word intuitively because he obviously was unaware of it at the time in any conscious way. Those of you who are aware of the remarkable relation between any two complementary hexachords will know that two hexachords which together contain all twelve pitch classes will always have the same intervallic content—the same intervallic content but not necessarily distributed the same way. The two hexachords in example 1-4 obviously have the same number of semitones, but the semitones are distributed in a different way: conjunctly in one, disjunctly in the other. They must have the same number of semitones and the same number of every other interval also. Look, for example, at the major seconds. There are two major seconds in each hexachord, but look at how differently they are distributed.

EXAMPLE 1-5

Such a difference in distribution would never be true of hexachords that are inversions of each other. I suspect that that's what really threw Schoenberg. He would look at the two hexachords from the Fourth Quartet or even from the Woodwind Quintet and realize that the intervals were all the same, with the same number of occurrences of each interval. Then he comes to the *Jakobsleiter* hexachords and realizes that they have a totally different distribution of the intervals. I'm convinced that Schoenberg thought that getting the same intervals on both sides of his set, when he divided it into two hexachords, was a property of his particular hexachords. When he could lay out his hexachord and then lay out the inversion and see that he was also getting complementary intervals, he felt great. But he got back to *Jakobsleiter* and couldn't do that, and he didn't recognize the fact that he was still getting the same interval multiplicities in both hexachords. And since he couldn't make them work the way his other hexachords had, he thought something must be haywire with the whole world. He thought that only very special hexachords had the property of having the same interval multiplicities as their complements. But that is not the case. It is true of any hexachord.

In *Jakobsleiter*, Schoenberg did manage to extract the same kind of motives from both hexachords, and, let's face it, that is the way he thought about it. My point is that in *Jakobsleiter* Schoenberg was already working intuitively with the combination of the motive and the complete chromatic. For example, he has ordered the trichords in these two very dissimilar hexachords so that all four trichords are the same trichord type. When he turned to the twelve-tone theme of *Jakobsleiter*, his problem wasn't a matter of using twelve-tone themes or using the complete chromatic. You can go back to the Opus 16, Number 3, orchestral piece or, even better, Opus 16, Number 1, and find that the notion of the complete chromatic—of eventually spanning the twelve chromatic pitch classes in a piece—is absolutely fundamental to the construction of a piece. Rather, the problem was related to the question of basically changing, hierarchically, the relationship between order and collection in music.

Now this has not often been written about because, first of all, it seems sort of cosmic. It's not cosmic; it's the way Schoenberg was thinking about a new way of writing music. I don't care how the genesis of the twelve-tone system is described. There's no doubt that, genetically, many of the operations of the system were suggested by the local motivic ideas in the music of the past. But once they are transformed over into the twelve-tone domain, they create a fundamentally different musical system. When I say that, I'm not speaking normatively; I'm not speaking qualitatively; rather I'm speaking purely analytically, descriptively.

Of course, you can argue with the premises. There was nothing obvious about what Schoenberg did. It was a remarkable step, and, though there may seem to have been all kinds of historical geneses and suggestions in Schoenberg's mind, once he made that step over the boundary, he was in a very new land indeed. It's too easy to bend over backwards and say, "Well, after all, it really wasn't that different." It *was* that different; and what has happened to music ever since, both positively and negatively, shows how fundamentally different it was. Schoenberg did try to find some new communality, but he did it only very relatively. People used to say, "Oh, the trouble with this new twelve-tone thing is it's too mechanistic; it tells you what to do." That's a preposterous statement. It is an absolute misrepresentation. If you've ever composed or ever decided to try writing twelve-tone music, you find that, as it turns out, it's like writing any other kind of music. You have to find out if it's for you or if it's not for you, how you think in it or how you hear in it.

The fact is, however, that twelve-tone music is much more contextual and much less communal than what anyone would call tonal music, whether you think of tonal music à la Rameau, à la Schenker, à la Kirnberger, or à la Schillinger. What is shared from one twelve-tone work to another twelve-tone work? There are not structures in common; there are just principles of formation and transposition. The contingencies and dependencies of the twelve-tone work are determined, in the very nature of its being a twelve-tone work, by the particular ordering of the twelve pitch classes in the particular work; and therefore, of course, to that extent a twelve-tone work is much more contextual than a tonal work, whose dependencies and contingencies remain the same in some respects not only within a work but also from work to work. If somebody goes through an elementary harmony course and plays example 1-6a for you and says, "It resolves as in example 1-6b," it's not a lie—it's a generalization of a rather simple kind.

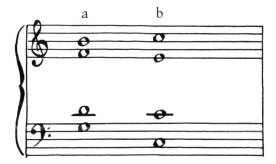

EXAMPLE 1-6

Those contingencies and dependencies do hold up through a tremendous amount of music. When you do first-species counterpoint or any species counterpoint the way I would like to see species counterpoint done (it could come from Fux or Schenker), you're dealing with contingencies and dependencies which underlie a tremendous amount of structural tonality.

Schoenberg was thinking also in terms of the structures of tonality, the structural functions (that's the name of his book on tonal harmony—*Structural Functions*[10]) in the twelve-tone sense. Well, these structural functions are all context dependent, dependent upon the ordering of the set. Let's talk about this issue of ordering just a little bit, as Schoenberg viewed it. (I'm afraid I may start mixing up the names of Schenker and Schoenberg: that's a psychological problem that I have. It's lucky Carnap doesn't come in—Carnap, Schenker, and Schoenberg are my Viennese triangle.) When Schoenberg began thinking about this, he thought about it intensively, and wrote, and tried, and sketched. The amount of work he did in notes is absolutely monumental. Schoenberg was not capable of deep theoretical thought; he hadn't been trained to do it. Generalized hexachordal theorems meant nothing to him. Every time he had to find one of his hexachords, he had to start from scratch again. He knew no general principles. On the other hand, his trial and error showed him a great deal as he proceeded. He learned a great deal about his specific materials because he knew no such generalizations.

Let me back up for a moment. One of Schoenberg's most basic ideas about tonal music was to see it in terms of collections. Depending upon how you view the tonal system or the tonal language or the tonal syntax, this conception of tonal music may be a little too crude, but, although it might differ in detail, I don't think it would violate yours in any serious way. You have, let's say, a C-major scale collection, and you move to another scale collection. One of the techniques of the composer is somehow to keep in mind constantly that one large tonality within which all else is framed. I'm talking now about the notion of a single tonality for a piece. (By the way, don't think this idea came from Schenker or was Schenker's alone. It came from Riemann, from Erpf; it came from all the stuff from which Schoenberg came.) When Schenker talked about tonicization rather than modulation, he was not fighting about terms for terms' sake—nobody finds the term *modulation* offensive. It's the question of what it connotes, and falsely connotes: the idea, for example, that the first theme of the *Eroica* Symphony is in E♭ and then the second theme is in B♭. I don't know whether people still say that anymore, but once people did. And the danger there is in just what may be misconstrued. Is that B♭ of that second theme the same as the B♭ of the first theme of the Fourth Symphony of Beethoven? Obviously not. You don't want to use the same terms for different functions. So in order to avoid misrepresenting the functions by using these terms, the idea of tonicization, of creating temporary tonics, is used because modulation always implies change of key. If at the end of a stock arrangement of *Melancholy Baby* you shift it up a half-step because the singer has to do it, that is a modulation!

In Schoenberg's *Structural Functions of Harmony* (which is hardly a revolutionary book; it's right out of Riemann) you have areas defined by scale structure. No one has ever minimized the ingenuity of the major scale structure (its unique multiplicity of interval and things of this kind which make all of these relationships possible), but it is above all a collection. No one speaks of ordering the scale. The scale is represented by its position finders (to use the language which has now become rather commonplace but is nevertheless useful). One can think of tonal music as proceeding from one collection through other collections, always maintaining the tonic area. These collections are projected by or modified by or defined by ordered themes and motives on the surface. Schoenberg's notion was one of areas that related to each other by virtue of tones in common or pitch classes in common, which were projected by ordered themes and ordered motives. Schoenberg would teach how you took a well-defined theme, how you reduced it to its components, neutralized it, re-formed other themes from it. This is what was called liquidation technique, and it's still taught at Barnard College, where there's someone who studied with Schoenberg at UCLA.[11] So Schoenberg's was a motivic conception which is always correlated with his notion of structural areas.

Let's see how these concepts apply in a twelve-tone context. Here is an ordering of the twelve pitch classes from Schoenberg's Fourth Quartet.

EXAMPLE 1-7

This happens to be a very special example; there's no other ordering like this in Schoenberg. All of his hexachords were like this in content, but no others were ordered like this. The hexachord of the Violin Concerto, which was written just before, has almost the same properties but not quite. This represents one peak of—I don't want to say complexity, I'd rather say richness. When you take a succession like this of pitch classes and you transpose it, that alone shows you how differently we have to think of hierarchization in these two musical domains. In tonal music, we can speak of hierarchization through the circle of fifths, through any number of rudimentary, but not trivial, concepts, which certainly are determinative. If you look at example 1-7, however, you suddenly realize that any transposition of this succession of twelve notes is going to give you just another succession of twelve notes. It's going to change not content but order. Now how can you possibly determine a general hierarchic organization of orderings? This is a new musical issue.

I hope nobody here thinks that we're talking about mathematics. If I really wanted to represent this set the way I should, I would write down 0, 11, 7, 8, 3, etc. The reason for that is not because these numbers make any mathematical sense—they don't. They have no virtues whatsoever. They're not even a

Fibonacci series! They represent nothing more than measures of interval. These numbers happen to be a real connection to the past. They function exactly the way numbers do in figured bass. They simply measure the intervals between pitch classes. When you write $^6_4$ under a bass note, all you're saying is count six diatonic steps and four diatonic steps above it. The numbers don't define the register; they don't define even the relationship of the note representing the six and the note representing the four. The numbers 0, 11, 7, 8, etc., are exactly the same. The music doesn't come from the numbers. The numbers come from trying to represent just that much of the music. These numbers represent a succession of pitch classes without any reference to register. Register is already contextual; register is ordering in space. That's another aspect of order that plays just as much a role in twelve-tone music as ordering in time, believe it or not. And there's no better example of that than the next little example (ex. 1-8a). We should look at the ordering of that theme from this point of view.

But before we do so, let me simply say this: it pleased Schoenberg (and Stravinsky too, when he saw the light) to write twelve-tone pieces. I knew Schoenberg very little. I knew Stravinsky very well. We were very close indeed—we were friends—and I lived very closely with him through the period in which he became enamored of all these ideas and forged for himself a very special technique. One of the remarkable things that Stravinsky said, when people felt that he had committed a treasonable act by starting to write pieces where you could find successions of twelve things like this at the beginning, was "There's nothing to it; I've always composed with intervals."[12] Now those of you who know the *Symphony of Psalms* or the *Symphony in Three Movements* will understand this. Basically, of course, it was something of a witticism, but what it did show, much more than a witticism, was how profoundly this is an interval kind of syntax and not just a pitch-class syntax—fundamentally and centrally an interval syntax.

When you transpose twelve pitch classes, you have a different ordering. How would you compare these orderings? As far as anybody has ever determined or demonstrated compositionally, there's no general principle. There's no question of notes in common, because you have all twelve pitch classes all the time. When Schoenberg was confronted by this problem, he was stuck on it a long time. He was not satisfied until he came up with a particular class of twelve-tone series (or sets or rows) which would keep a collection fixed. That was the master stroke; it allowed for a change of both notions of hierarchization: not only that of the relationship between order and collection, but also among the orderings themselves. I'm not saying this is a necessary condition for twelve-tone music to be good, intelligible, or coherent or anything else, but for him it was. It became a universal of his twelve-tone music. If you invert a set of this type and transpose it by a certain interval, you get a collection which remains fixed (and of course the complementary one must also remain fixed). However, the internal ordering of each collection is changed: the resultant set is a permutation.

I want to talk about register for a moment. Schoenberg and Stravinsky both loved the idea of setting out in a specific explicit foreground form an ordering of twelve pitch classes where the register is terribly important. Then suddenly this ordering recedes from the surface. The twelve-tone set, depending on how it's laid out at the beginning, becomes the determinant not just of local thematic, contrapuntal, or harmonic events. It becomes the determinant of the progression and structure of the piece. But it can recede so far from the foreground that you may never be aware of it explicitly. It may never ever return explicitly. It recedes and acts at constantly varying distances. This results in (although this is very hard to document) an extraordinary reach and richness of relatedness and depth of reference.

Let's go back to the opening measures of the Fourth Quartet. The layout of register shows a high degree of determinacy, of trying to make everything count musically. This doesn't mean using some abstract notion of what counts, but relating things to the piece internally, or—there we are again—contextually. Here are the first six notes of the Fourth Quartet as they are laid out in the first violin.

EXAMPLE 1-8a

After stating his first hexachord, which he articulates very obviously, he then lays out the next six notes of his set in a particular registral distribution which is the only one out of the six-factorial (6!) registral distributions which will define a particular relationship between the two hexachords which is fundamental to the structure of the piece, the counterpoint of the piece, the progression of the piece.

EXAMPLE 1-8b

This is musical! Don't look for formulas and don't look for arithmetical tricks. Purely musical criteria are found. I'm simply claiming or avowing that all we're dealing with here are musical issues. The primitives are the same as in tonal music. We're talking about pitch; we're talking pitch class.

When we began using the term *pitch class*, it was looked upon as the word of a clique. There are so many things that happened in contemporary music, particularly with Schoenberg: his music of the present made us rethink many of our ways of thinking about music of the past. The word *pitch class* is not something that shouldn't have been used or couldn't have been used much earlier. For example, if I say to you, "What is the tonic of the Fifth Symphony of Beethoven?" you could say, "C." But which C? Is this C the tonic?

EXAMPLE 1-9

It's really a class of tonics we're referring to.

Many of the confusions in Schenker, by the way, are because he often doesn't discriminate between pitch class and pitch. You're never quite sure what he means, and this results in some obscurity. It's like the question of register. We're constantly talking about being in the same register, but let's think about it more closely. What does it mean to be in the same register— say, for two notes to be in the same register? We suddenly realize that this gets us into a very complicated and obscure situation. If I should ask you if these two notes (ex. 1-10a) are in the same register, you'd probably say yes.

EXAMPLE 1-10

Well, then, these two (ex. 1-10b) therefore have to be in the same register, right? Well, so, are these two (ex. 1-10c) in the same register? It's not a transitive relation. When do you stop being in the same register? I wouldn't mind a rather sophisticated notion that eventually perhaps a piece becomes all one register—a perfectly reasonable point of view. One simply has to think about these things. You simply cannot say "in the same register" in a nonacoustical sense without dealing in something highly contextual and very fuzzy.

Let's get back to the Fourth Quartet and the relationship between the hexachords. When somebody says, "Can you hear these things?" the answer is that it's not a matter of hearing. Of course, you can hear these different notes. "Hearing" is one of those expressions that seems to represent a high degree of humanistic professionalism. But it's not a matter of hearing; it's a matter of the way you think it through conceptually with your musical mind. You can hear those six notes in example 1-8a. You hear where they are in register. You would certainly hear the contour difference if I played the hexachord in example 1-8b with the F♯ an octave higher than it is written. You'd hear everything. So it's not a matter of whether you hear it, it's a matter of how you conceptualize it, how you conceive it.

Let's arpeggiate the first hexachord from bottom to top and then arpeggiate the second hexachord from top to bottom.

EXAMPLE 1-11

Do you see what Schoenberg has done? He's made it clear in his registral distribution that the second collection is an inversion of the first collection, which is by no means trivial. By so distributing it in register, he's telling you that there's going to be a particular relationship between the hexachord and its inversion which will create aggregates, that is, complete twelve-tone collections in which the segments of the two sets will be so used. This is the way Schoenberg's music goes. It's not the only way it goes; it's one of the many ways it goes. It's the idea of constantly intimating where you are going—constantly predicting so that when you arrive in certain places in the piece, you have the sense of having gotten someplace which has already been predicted. People talk about directed motion. It's one of these virtuous statements about tonal music. Well *this* is directed motion. It's being directed *within* the piece rather than by any universal principles—and I'm not so sure about universal principles anyhow.

This is where I come from—a notion of the music of Schoenberg. Not so much from Stravinsky, because I was a twelve-tone composer before he was, but more so (though much more systematically than musically) from Webern. Webern's music was for me much more suggestive than rich—I'm a Schoenbergite. If I have to choose between Schoenberg's and Webern's music, I choose Schoenberg's, without question. I always have. That's a statement of personal disposition. Schoenberg was a much more striking phenomenon for me—the idea of this hermetically sealed music by a hermetically sealed man. For those of us who aspired to write a certain kind of music, Schoenberg's was much more of an ideal of music. And I don't mean technically. The combination of Webern and Schoenberg is absolutely crucial to me. It turned out that what they were doing quite separately converged for me at a certain point where they become eminently related without being intimately related. Each staked out his own little domain.

The other part of this Viennese group (and remember, the only one I knew personally at all was Schoenberg, so it has nothing to do with personalities) was Berg, who was probably the most misunderstood of the group. Berg was the real intellectual of the crowd. You may say, "Was his music intellectual?" Well, that the mind works when one writes music is something I take for granted. Of course there is mindless music, but that's not what we're talking about. Webern's music is sonically very striking and grows out of a very special idea of chromatic completion. But Berg wrote the music which was always used to batter poor Schoenberg. Berg was the "real composer." His music sounded like "real music"—particularly the Violin Concerto (when they were still performing it), *Der Wein* (which would sometimes get performed), or the *Lyric Suite*. In fact, Berg's structures in *Lulu*, the Violin Concerto, *Der Wein*, and the *Lyric Suite* have things so recondite that they sometimes make you wonder, again, not can you hear them, but rather, can you conceptualize them?

Out of all this came more or less the generalizations that are mine. Now I remain therefore an unreconstructed and not-have-to-be-born-again twelve-tone composer. I haven't been talking about my music explicitly, because I thought this would give you more of an insight. For example, I could tell you that I took the notion of the Schoenbergian hexachord and I generalized it. And it turns out that when you generalize it, it relates to something that

Webern did, such as making a trichord play a very fundamental musical role. The trichord is the minimal structure which can reflect the transformations of twelve-tone thinking, and the relation between the two becomes intimate in ways that one can never suspect. Let me show you: here is the beginning of the *Concerto for Nine Instruments* of Webern (ex. 1-12). I'm not putting these in the correct register, not for what we're going to be talking about. I'm just writing out the pitch classes and representing them by pitches.

EXAMPLE 1-12

The *Concerto for Nine Instruments* is one of my most unfavorite pieces—it's too literal for me. It's not my cup of tea musically at all. But it was fundamentally suggestive for me. Webern takes this first trichord and simply applies the interval-preserving transformations. That, of course, is the point that Stravinsky was making. Intervals are preserved. The retrograde inversion, which is considered so remote from musical reality, turns out to be the simplest thing in the world. No matter the transposition level, the retrograde inversion reverses the intervals. It's interval invariant. This twelve-note succession consists of a trichord, the retrograde inversion of the trichord, the retrograde, and the inversion.

P   RI   R   I

EXAMPLE 1-13

The trichord thus generates a twelve-tone series. Now that is a very different kind of conception. It's within the twelve-tone conception, but you apply the operations not to induce permutations (changes of order) but to induce a generation of a set.

    It turns out that there are deep ramified relations between the sets that these trichords generate and those comprised of such hexachords as we were talking of. Indeed the Schoenberg Fourth Quartet uses trichords too, not in this way but in another way, to create associations. There are always multiple chains of relationships developed by the segments of the individual orderings of each transformation of the set. That's why order is so important. From the standpoint of collection these four trichords are absolutely identical and create absolutely no differentiations whatsoever. From the standpoint of order, they're utterly different and therefore, of course, can be referred to and used in explicit and individual ways.

One of your classmates has been digging through my *Minute Waltz*, trying to find the twelve-tone series, or set, or row, and she wasn't quite sure where it was. This reflects on so many of the subjects here, some of which I regard as less crucial and some of which are rather large, but I thought I'd be historical: she reminded me of something which is true and I'll start with that. Right after the *Three Compositions for Piano* and before *Du*, I wrote a piece called *Composition for Four Instruments*. Now the *Composition for Four Instruments* was the first piece of mine that got around a great deal. *Three Compositions for Piano* didn't because they're rather difficult to play. *Composition for Four Instruments* was played very early in my career, right after the war, and was the first piece of mine to be published. Therefore it got into the hands of people, and, above all, it got into the hands of an expert. Now what happened was that this expert wrote me finally one day and said, "Look, I've got a score and a tape of this piece, but where the hell is the row, or the series?"

The question reflected a notion which had been prevalent in the thirties that you write out the twelve notes as a kind of theme and then you do funny things to them. The notion that it has anything to do with skill, continuity, structure, imitation, any of the things which would be taken for granted within a few years was simply not imaginable. There was, for example, associated with this, another kind of argument. The thirties were a rather turbulent era. People were very much concerned about political matters, so the big argument was that the great virtue (and this was argued by rather eminent composers) of the twelve-tone series was its inherent democracy, since every note is free and equal. One note, one vote! In fact there was talk like that on a more serious plane. And then of course some more intelligent person would say, "How can any twelve notes be all equal? One's going to be longer, one's going to be higher, one's going to be first, one's going to be last." That was considered really a demanding question. But, again, this was all said. There was a wonder of all this, and the anarchy of all this. That was the atmosphere of things. You do have to realize this. Even the friendliest of people were totally and utterly baffled. And they became resentful as baffled people so often do.

Now I get back to my own experiences in 1948. My *Composition for Four Instruments* begins with an unaccompanied clarinet solo. I'm now going to write out exactly what the first clarinet plays unaccompanied at the beginning of the piece, including the rests.

EXAMPLE 1-14

Now, of course, if you start counting (and then take off your shoes to get those extra two) they all add up to twelve. But I don't have to say more than once that twelve is not important, the *effect* of the twelve is. You have twelve different pitch classes represented in the specific registral placement. This is what led that expert (and I'm not using the term lightly; he had had a lot of experience with this—he had studied with Ernst Krenek) to say to me, "Look, I give up. I've been looking at the piece for nine months and I don't know what to say." And of course my response to that was, "That's not the way I conceive of a set. This is not a matter of finding the lost set. This is not a matter of cryptoanalysis (where's the hidden set?). What I'm interested in is the effect it might have, the way it might assert itself not necessarily explicitly." Always throughout this piece, for example, it's there in a very decisive way. It's continuously, thoroughly, and utterly influential, but in constantly different ways and in constantly different degrees of explicitness and acting at various distances from the surface of the piece. Now the reason I say this is because it never occurred to me when I was writing this piece that anyone would ask this question. I regarded this as a very simple, direct piece. With *Three Compositions* and with this piece, though, I wasn't writing "for an audience"; I was still very much aware of the fact that I was writing a music that very few people, including professionals, had had experience with, aurally or in any other sense. So therefore it never occurred to me that the

27 The Twelve-Tone Tradition

big issue would be what the set of the piece was. I had no idea that anyone would misconstrue the opening clarinet solo as being necessarily the set of the piece any more than one necessarily thinks that, because the first thing you hear in the First Symphony of Beethoven is an F-major triad, the piece is therefore to be construed as in F major.

By setting up the first trichord and isolating it from the rest, I thought that would set up the assumption, the premise, the theme for this continuity. The continuity would be very clearly displayed by the delineation in the lower register of a trichord which is obviously the inversion of the first trichord. Similarly, the retrograde of the first trichord is isolated in the upper register and the retrograde inversion is in between.

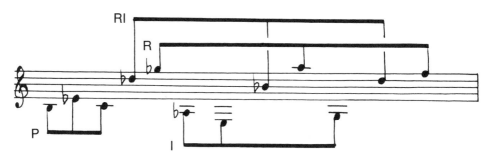

EXAMPLE 1-15

If I didn't know to whom I was speaking, I would never use the term *retrograde inversion*; I would just point out that the intervals are repeated. *Retrograde inversion*, after all, like so many of the terms we use, is just an abbreviational indication of a primitive property. The whole thing, of course, adds up to a twelve-tone aggregate which has been ordered compositionally, ordered contextually on the surface, to give you an alternate set. Example 1-14 is a kind of chromatic thematic surface underneath which would be the properties of another ordered set. The notion is of that ordering as a referential source far deeper than that which appears on the immediate surface.

Let me speak briefly about my Second Quartet. It's a very early piece of mine, relatively speaking, when you consider when I started—restarted—composing again; it was written in 1953. That's thirty years ago, which is even for me a few years. The piece begins like this.

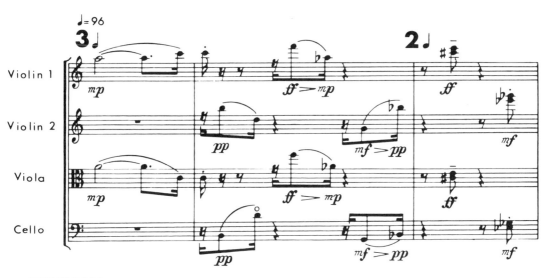

EXAMPLE 1-16

It begins with unisons and octaves. An opening trichord is very explicit, but if you were looking for a twelve-tone set, you'd have trouble. Now I don't say that with any degree of pride. For me, from almost the beginning, the notion was that of a structural influence, far more than explicit statement.

Starting in measure 7 you get a set derived from the trichord A–C–Ab.

EXAMPLE 1-17

29 The Twelve-Tone Tradition

This is the same trichord as the first violin and viola had *mezzo piano* in measures 1–2 (see ex. 1-16). Towards the end of the piece, the four instruments play a line in unison.

EXAMPLE 1-18

This is the first explicit statement of the series in the piece. But notice that the pitch level at the beginning of the piece is determined by what happens here at the end of the piece. The pitch level of the first trichord in measure 7 was chosen so that the hexachord derived from it (A–C–Ab/B–G–Bb) will give you the same hexachord collection as the first hexachord of that explicit statement of the complete series at the end of the piece (see ex. 1-18). More explicitly, the first trichord in measure 7 (A–C–Ab) together with the retrograde inversion of that trichord (B–G–Bb) gives you a certain hexachord. The first and second trichords of the complete series are not the same trichord type, but the first hexachord of the complete series and the first hexachord in measure 7 have the same pitch-class content. In other words, the pitch level of the hexachord of the fundamental series influences how I choose the pitch level of the first trichord in the derivational form of measure 7ff. This is an important point for me: the series is in there exerting its influence constantly without being explicitly present.

QUESTION: Had you studied Schoenberg's music before he came to America?

Yes, I had, as a matter of fact, by historical accident. I was interested in his music and in Stravinsky's music. It's very simply biographical—the way things happen, the way our lives become totally and utterly wrecked at very early stages. Misspent infancy. I would be doing something civilized otherwise. When I was about ten years old, my mother was in Philadelphia very often, and I was involved with people who were around the Curtis Institute. Curtis was a very different place at that time, and I knew an extraordinary man named Paul Nordoff, whose name I'm always happy to mention because he's been so long forgotten—an extraordinary man who could play eight modern concerti at the drop of his fingers; he was a genius of a very special type.[13] From him, I heard the Opus 11 pieces of Schoenberg. I didn't know what to make of this music, but even as a kid I became interested in it. Of course, I was in music very much, but mainly I was either playing "On Wisconsin" in bands in the South, or playing in little orchestras, or making arrangements and playing pop music and jazz. This other music was so different, such an absolutely different world, that I became very interested. I was not a pianist, but I got these pieces and also the Stravinsky Piano Sonata. Then, later, I got hold of Webern's little pieces for cello and piano, which I tried to imitate; they're not as imitable as I had thought. The answer is yes, I was very much a Schoenbergite. Even at that time, even that young. That's another of the reasons I went to New York at the time I went.

QUESTION: What were you doing in the late thirties?

When I got out of college in 1935, Schoenberg had already left New York. I couldn't go to study with Schoenberg in California. And, really, I had seen enough of Schoenberg to know that he would not talk about twelve-tone music. Schoenberg, for example, could not play the piano even as much as I do (he certainly couldn't play cocktail music as much as I), and he wouldn't go to the piano at all. He would stand at the blackboard and he'd say, "Mr. Stein, play a C-major triad."[14] He absolutely refused to go near the piano. He was very embarrassed about his inability to play the piano at all. The reason I tell you that is he would not say anything about twelve tones. Leonard Stein said that when you'd come for a lesson with him and he'd be working on his own music, he would immediately put it away. That's all part of the milieu. He had his secrets and he wasn't going to reveal them. Both he and Stravinsky had the notion that somehow they endowed their music with secrets that made the music as great as it was—but you could never infer them from studying the music itself. Very funny for us, but not funny for them.

So I went and studied with Roger Sessions for a couple of years. He was very anti-Schoenberg. We mainly did Schenker analysis and we did species counterpoint—he tore up my music whenever he saw it. Then he, too, changed his ways, as you know. The fact is that we became very close, and when he went to Princeton, I went there a little bit later. I wrote a lot of music during that period. To demonstrate that I could write music, I even won a Bearns Prize for something called *Music for the Mass*, which was sort of Hindemithian. What Roger Sessions would make us do, for example, is study a Mozart string quartet and then write an imitation movement—not imitating the thematic materials or the so-called form in terms of some sort of pattern of recurrences but, rather, what we felt was important about the piece, reconstructing it in our own terms, but still more or less in the Mozart idiom. We did enormous amounts of that kind of thing. My first actual large-scale twelve-tone pieces were some songs which have gotten lost. They got lost during the war—it's just one of those things.

2 Contextual Counterpoint

I'm going to get into some pretty hairy technical things during this session, merely because they do reflect things that are going on in the music. Some of these things will come up as we look at the second movement of the Webern *Piano Variations*. Later, we can look at an interesting gloss on that movement. I didn't produce this gloss, but I'm going to show you the obvious aspects of it. Then I'm going to ask you if you can see that the composer who did produce it has added something which is very nonintuitive, which is rather a remarkable nonobvious property of inversional relationships in time. It's a temporal rhythmic question which suggests all kinds of things about what can remain constant throughout a piece and what is so dependent upon order.

I want to begin by reminding you of the way Webern used, almost explicitly, those properties which maintain between an ordering and its inversion. I am speaking now of an ordering of the total chromatic, without which some of the properties are simply lost. It's a general inversional principle, but you need the total chromatic to get certain specific properties.

EXAMPLE 2-1

Example 2-1 shows the canonic opening of Webern's *Piano Variations*, Opus 27, second movement. There are bound to be two notes fixed since this

33

is an even transpositional relationship, and they're bound to be a tritone apart (marked with asterisks on the example). We also know that there's bound to be one and only one dyad, occurring twice, which will be the same each time in both interval and pitch content, and here the two occurrences happen to be next to each other, which is undoubtedly the way Webern arranged it (marked with double daggers on the example). The fixed notes and the fixed tritones are the features from which it all starts. Let me also remind you that Webern begins a repeat of the canon by starting on one of these fixed notes.

EXAMPLE 2-2

Now if I wanted to be very fancy, I could also say that what he's really doing is retaining the index number through all these four statements of the canon. Do you think you're all set on that, if I may use the expression? The idea of index number seems like just a numerical thing, but it has ramifications far beyond the local. We're bound to look first at the local manifestations because this is the easiest way to understand them, as they appear in a piece. And when I talk about further manifestations, you're likely to be a little skeptical. I'm going to try to overcome some of that skepticism today. Index number has exactly the same relationship to inversional hierarchization as interval number does to transpositional hierarchization. A total transposition of example 2-1 would obviously begin with interval 2, followed by interval 0, followed by interval 8, and so on. But that's not what he does. He transposes the individual lines literally, but by different transposition numbers while maintaining the index number. With G♯ as pitch class 0, the index number is 2. Of course it doesn't make any difference what pitch class you assign the 0 since it's a movable *do* system. If you prefer a fixed *do* system with C = 0, then in this case the index number would be 6.

So, when the piece continues (see ex. 2-2), Webern begins on the octave E♭s and transposes each set—to repeat the canon, if you wish. But he repeats the canon with the criterion that I don't think would have made very much sense in any pre-twelve-tone serial day. He repeats the canon retaining the dyads and, therefore, retaining the index numbers. The upper part in example 2-1 began on Bb and ended on Eb, while the lower part went from Ab to Eb. Therefore when the canon repeats, the upper part will go from Eb to Ab, while the lower goes from Eb to Bb. (Everybody has his own technique for getting screwed up playing this piece; the problem comes about because of a neat little trick at the end, which the middle prepares you for, as we will see.)

One of the most characteristic aspects of Webern's technique in these *Piano Variations*, which he expands in the *Variations* Opus 30, is to use the same index number for every single variation in the piece. I don't think he discovered it by generalizing about index number, by taking a collection and talking about index number the way we do. He, however, saw immediately that if he began with any dyad of the first set (as he did with the Ebs at the beginning of example 2-2) and then transposed both sets to retain that dyad, he would retain all the same pitch dyads. Notice, however, that this does rather radical things to certain aspects of the music. But I think there's nothing—and you know how I dislike this kind of generalization—but there's almost nothing more characteristic of what Webern, Schoenberg, and others of us have been up to than recognizing the high degree of contextuality. One of the things with which you have to grapple is what's going to remain fixed throughout a piece or throughout a passage of a piece and what's going to vary, how it's going to vary, and where these correlations are going to change. That becomes part of the rhythm of the piece.

I have never written a piece within the past twenty years that I didn't get letters about in which people say, "I'm sorry but there are 4,892 mistakes in your piece." And I do get lots like that from young composers. Maybe one or two of them are right; there are misprints or miscopying or something. But mainly they incorrectly assume if the piece starts a certain way, it has to go that way, that's all. Part of the notion of the piece may have been that certain things change their dependencies, their contingencies, and their relationships in the course of the piece. Things change!

Let me make a rough analogy. In a tonal piece, you might suddenly find yourself tonicized in some area other than where you started. If you were in C, the B would normally go to C. If you tonicize V, however, the B is suddenly the third degree of what is the temporary tonic. Would you then say that the B is not resolving correctly? It's very much the same kind of thing. So we have, again, typical examples of how you get both constancy and alteration.

Notice that what was the fifth dyad in example 2-1 becomes the second dyad in example 2-2. The order of pitch dyads changes, but the pitch dyads themselves remain fixed. Therefore what you get is a new kind of rhythm. What makes the playing of this piece usually sound like a typewriter performance (it's very hard to find a good performance of it) is that the pianists usually don't manage to infuse the performance with these rhythmic changes that take place. Some of you will recognize Webern's hexachord as a very familiar hexachord; it's a good old chromatic hexachord. And with a chromatic hexachord he could have made the passage combinatorial and made an aggregate, but (just the reverse of what he does in the *Cantata*) he chooses a transpositional level so there's only one note in common. Thus in both example 2-1 and example 2-2 the upper line and the lower line have one note in common in the first half and one note in common in the second half, each time A or E♭.

I'm being sloppy about my language. I should say *pitch class* rather than *note*, but as long as there's no misunderstanding, I'll use the shortest possible expression. There are two ways in which Webern is dealing with dyads. The first is based upon the fact that there is no tritone in his hexachord. That means that there cannot be a repetition of an interval within the section of the piece, because only elements a tritone apart will have the same interval under inversion. I'm going to number the intervals 1 through 6 (see ex. 2-3). Interval #1 is two semitones; interval #2 is a unison; interval #3 is eight semitones; and so on.

EXAMPLE 2-3

Notice that after interval #6 they begin to repeat, but in a different order. In the second half of example 2-3, interval #6 comes first, followed by interval #4, and so on. What he's getting is a permutation of the actual intervals. This constitutes one level on which things change. The other level, of course, has to do with actual pitch content. Let's number the pitch dyads 1 through 6 (see ex. 2-4). Pitch dyad #1 is G♯–B♭; pitch dyad #2 is A–A; and so on.

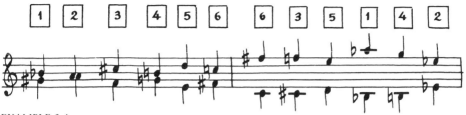

EXAMPLE 2-4

As with the actual intervals, the pitch dyads (with the exception of the fixed pitches A) all repeat in the second half of the example but not in the same order as in the first half. He has set up his original hexachord so that he has these exclusivities operating on these six dyads in two different ways—as pitch dyads and as interval dyads. I don't want to belabor this anymore except to point out to you that when the piece continues, all of the orders of all of the dyads change. If you compare examples 2-1 and 2-2, you will see that the fifth dyad (E–D) becomes the second, the seventh (C–F♯) becomes the third, and so on. Everything changes from a standpoint of dyadic order. What doesn't change, of course, is that C is still against the F♯, E against the D, and so on. Now, one might say, "Well you're really only talking about a very limited kind of property. You're talking about a sort of first-species property, and although Webern wrote some note-against-note pieces, who else would want to do so?"

What I'm going to show you are the extensions of this which remove it far from the note-against-note category. Having gotten to the point in the music represented by the end of example 2-2, Webern gets the dyad Bb–Ab, but by writing the repeat sign, his hands reverse. He takes off from the same place again and does just what he did before. After repeating the music represented by examples 2-1 and 2-2, he picks up the last dyad of example 2-2 (Bb–Ab) and uses it to begin a new repetition of his double canon. This time, of course, the lines are each transposed at a different level, but he still retains his index numbers so the Eb is against the Eb as it was before; the B against the G as it was before; and so on. But he's got a problem. At this transposition level, he's going to end up on a Db in the upper line and an F in the lower. He doesn't write long pieces, and he's got a circle of fifths going. The upper line, from the beginning, goes from Bb to Eb (ex. 2-1); from Eb to Ab (ex. 2-2); from Ab to Db as the piece continues. How do you stop without writing out the whole thing? Well, here's how he stops. Back at the double bar, he set up a precedent of crossing the voices. In the second half of the piece, he crosses the voices again. In the final statement, the F takes him back to B♭, while the D♭, of course, will take him to A♭. And he's back where he started, on B♭ and A♭, which is good enough to end any piece. Now this may just look like a cute gimmick. But within that conception of how you round off a piece, remember again that all of these dyads are going to remain fixed. There are twelve different index numbers, and if he wanted to, he could have gone through all twelve, each of which would have given him a radical and discernible difference in the order of pitch dyads.

The gloss I referred to earlier is a piano piece by Dallapiccola called "Contrapunctus Secundus" from his *Quaderno Musicale di Annalibera*. It's strange to think of Dallapiccola doing this kind of thing. It's not what is usually associated with him. Of course, Dallapiccola wrote nothing but canons—virtually every piece of his is a canon. There's a long article on his technique of canon by John Perkins.[1] Let me show you what Dallapiccola did.

EXAMPLE 2-5

He has exactly the same number of parts as Webern and has the canon statement four times, but he uses a rather different set of properties in the second half. He begins with exactly the same interval although he uses a very different kind of hexachord. These pieces were written for his daughter and have very distinct technical limitations because they are basically for a child to play. Also, Dallapiccola changed some things and made the final version cuter. If any of you have a chance to hear the first piano version, you might find it fun to test yourself and see what he changed later. Now, notice that he does exactly what Webern does. C comes against C, which suggests, of course, that F♯ has to come against F♯. You see already one of the aspects of a trick developing. What Webern took as the fixed tritone, Dallapiccola takes as the fixed notes, and what Webern took as the fixed notes, he takes as the fixed tritone. Therefore if A is against E♭, then E♭ must be against A. You can't have one without the other. That's where already you begin to get the sense that you're dealing with a gloss.

Now, when he begins the second statement, he does exactly what Webern did.

EXAMPLE 2-6

I don't mean, by the way, that he repeats the last note. That was Webern-esque. Dallapiccola wouldn't have done that. That would have been too obvious. But he does exactly the same thing as Webern with regard to retaining the dyads and the index numbers. The rest of the canon follows exactly the same principle from the standpoint of note-against-note. Dallapiccola simply reverses the roles of the tritones—the tritones as fixed notes and the tritones as repeated dyadic tritones with the same total pitch content. So he goes ahead and repeats with the same index numbers and therefore gets the same dyads. I think he wanted to get this because of things that happen in other pieces. Notice also that he begins and ends with the tritone—that is very Dallapiccolan. He was trying, of course, to incorporate some of his own ideas about how to close the canon.

He begins the second part with a Bb in the upper line and an Ab in the lower.

EXAMPLE 2-7

That, of course, was the initial dyad of the Webern. But now you can say, "Hey, he's deserted the whole principle. He's deserted the principle of maintaining his index numbers because the Bb and the Ab are not dyads in the first two sections." Now comes the fun. What do you think you might do if you were thinking along these sorts of fun lines of writing a piece like this? What is this going to yield? First, look at the rather minor trick that he pulls, and then we'll worry about the larger issues. The E♭s now come together the way E♭s did in the Webern. If the E♭s come together here, we know very well that the As must come together. So the notes that were, before, the notes that were used as the repeating tritones now become the fixed notes, exactly as they were in the Webern. You can already see, therefore, what's going to happen. The C is going to come out opposite F♯. And if C is opposite F♯, F♯ would be opposite the C. That's pretty cute because, of course, now he's gotten back to the Webern by interchanging the role of the fixed notes and the fixed tritones, which is one step beyond what Webern did: he kept all of that fixed throughout the piece. That's what he did with the Webern and the things which are explicitly related to the Webern. But he did something much more subtle.

You may infer that what we've been discussing is a very limited property, but I'm going to show you how general it is. It has to do with the relationship between inversions, which you never think of as being a temporal or rhythmic relationship, and the rhythmic implications of inversion. Suppose you just listen to what goes on harmonically in the music—the successive intervals.

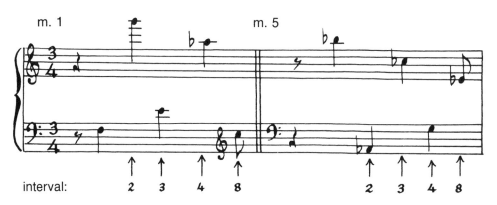

EXAMPLE 2-8

The canon that starts in measure 1 begins with the interval succession 2–3–4–8. The canon beginning in measure 5 has totally different pitches—it retains only those tritone-associated notes—but it still begins with interval succession 2–3–4–8. We're getting exactly the same interval succession with totally different pitches. This is a property of inversion which is absolutely general—it doesn't have to be note-against-note or anything else. I could have presented this to you as an abstract property which is pretty startling. But here is a simple example of it, note-against-note. As long as we keep the rhythmic relation between two voices the same, we can transpose them to any level we wish, and the intervals will remain the same. There's nothing trivial about that. They're not the same notes.

Now I want to show you this property in general. Let's take a totally different series or set and do it in the most general sense. Let's take the series from the familiar Fourth Quartet of Schoenberg (who never did anything of the sort). The intuitive basis of this is not at all obvious, because it's not the way one normally thinks about the effects of inversion. I could use the combinatorial inversion but I won't, because you might think there's something special about that. So to avoid any misunderstandings, I'm just going to take an arbitrary inversional level of 9 and write the two set forms quite arbitrarily rhythmically—no note-against-note or anything of that kind.

EXAMPLE 2-9

By the way, this property has nothing to do with hexachords. You can do it with three notes, for example. The two sets don't both have to have the same number of notes. The generality of it is quite remarkable. What I'm asserting is as follows: I take two inversionally related lines, related by any interval, with any temporal relations whatsoever between them. I then maintain only the relative temporal relation. Now please observe that the interval succession in both parts of example 2-9 is 3–2–9–10–6–1–2. Think of what a compositional device this is or, if you wish, what a compositional treasure, resource. You may test it if you wish and discover that you don't have to restrict this to two voices. You can use four, six, eight, ten, twenty-four voices, as long as you maintain the original inversional relationships.

Now can you possibly intuit why this should happen? I don't want you to think that it's some gag or some tautology—there's nothing obvious about it. We're getting the same intervals, but not the same pitches. Notice that the

9 is made by either E–C♯ or C–A. The 10 is made first by E♭ and C♯ and then by C and B♭. The pitches are different. That's why Dallapiccola could transpose his lines and still get the same intervallic succession. The pitch level has nothing to do with it.

Contrapuntally, there's a kind of contextual counterpoint—a kind of associative counterpoint. Once you have these two voices going one against the other—whatever the basis is for choosing these intervals (probably there'd be some other compositional basis, given all the other things that can happen in a piece)—you can reverse their temporal relationship at any pitch level and still come out with the same interval succession but with totally different pitches. This is a very deep property. You'd be surprised at how often fragments of this turn up in pieces, where the composer has obviously seen that this is happening in his piece. It's very seldom generalized, however. The Dallapiccola example is, of course, obviously derived from the knowledge that this is going to happen in general—and he does use it in lots of other pieces. We could pursue this, but we don't have to. Once you've seen these specific compositional instances, you can see the extent to which the property can be extended and generalized.

Now I want to consider a famous example from the Webern *Symphony.* The second movement of the Webern *Symphony* begins with a theme stated in the clarinet.

EXAMPLE 2-10

This passage is almost impossible to hear on recordings, by the way, for reasons of balance. The old Craft recording certainly didn't work, and the Boulez is not much better. In this passage, Webern creates little aggregates. He accompanies the clarinet with the harp and horns playing the set in retrograde, so of course, you get automatic and trivial aggregates. (When I say trivial, by the way, I don't mean the music is trivial. I mean these would be true of any set anywhere; you can always create aggregates of this type.) Notice that he's using the same hexachord that he used in the *Piano Variations*—the chromatic hexachord; here, however, he uses it very differently.

Now let's consider the horn variation (Variation 2).

EXAMPLE 2-11

There are aspects of this passage which were extremely suggestive to later composers, many of whom are still alive. Notice first that the horn has an inversional canon.

EXAMPLE 2-12

This is another way in which Webern does the same thing he did in the *Piano Variations,* you might say even more literally, note-against-note. The canon is projected metrically, rather than instrumentally or registrally, through the notes which occur on the "strong" part of the beat. That's why the meter is 2/4, not 4/8. Once again, we have all these note-against-note inversions. One of the interesting aspects of the canon is that it reverses F–E/E–F. If F is against E (as it is in measure 1), E has to be against F (as it is in measure 4); we know that from our fairly routine constancies with regard to inversion.

The idea that meter can project a pitch-class line allows for a real counterpoint here, but notice that the surface pitch-class order is no longer the order of the series. Anybody who goes along here trying to count up to twelve is in trouble. The idea that you can't repeat a note until you've heard all twelve notes is nothing but a legend; obviously you can't count up to twelve here. But you can see something that becomes a terribly important principle for Schoenberg, which is not usually associated with Webern, however. I'm referring to the combination of two forms of the set in such a way as to produce some other kind of structure which relates to the original set. Notice, for example, how you get these orderings which have nothing to do with the original set; for example, F–E–D itself (see the asterisk in example 2-11), that little trichord, is not even present in the original set. One can go much farther than that. Certainly G–D–G–E♭ (see the double dagger in example 2-11) is not present; it couldn't possibly be. In other words, we begin to see here what the aggregate provides: a way for keeping constant certain segments of ordering. Here, you're not abandoning the ordering which is the referential norm for the piece. Rather, you're taking that ordering and expanding it by combinations which obviously yield relationships which are bound not to be in the original ordering of the segments, because of the fact that the intervals which are not present in the individual hexachords are bound to be present when you combine the remaining pitch classes. (As an aside, this leads to what a trill means in Webern's music. A trill will always represent two different voices converging, because otherwise the ordering would be arbitrarily disturbed. There are not many trills in Webern's music.) But look at something else. This is a canon projected by metrical position. Webern takes the first note of the movement and uses that as the first note of the inversion. That's very familiar for Webern, but why does he start the second canonic voice on E?

To consider this question, we must consider obvious musical pitch identities. This perception is a matter of conceptualization. I still encounter people who say, "But can you hear this?" Well obviously that's not the right question. Obviously you can hear these things—you hear the notes. The question is how you conceive them, how you conceptualize them, how you relate them. It's not a matter of hearing in any physiological or discriminatory sense. It's not a matter of perception in any crude sense, though obviously there's no such thing as crude perception (but that's another story). Psychologically, I find it fascinating that one doesn't focus in on certain things.

But to return to Webern, do you notice what he's done? Why did he choose that interval? Everything we've said so far would be just as true if he had begun that canon on F–D♭–F–D♭. Why choose that E? You could perfectly well answer, "Well, hell. He had to choose something." But on the other hand, there's a well-defined relationship there, one that you'll immediately see, hear, and adore. Just look, just listen.

ANSWER: The first six pitch classes of the horn part form the hexachord of the original series.

Exactly, thank you. And that's the only pitch level at which he could have done that. You can regard this as invoking a harmonic principle. We've talked already about a contrapuntal principle: he is running two set forms, one against the other, as in example 2-12. (Notice, by the way, that he even repeats the notes, as he did in the theme.) All of that could be regarded as contrapuntal. But what subsumes them? What contains them? What contains them is the hexachord. So he's using the content of the first hexachord of the original set to determine new combinations which are not bound by any principle except the one of making further associations and exploiting them. By starting the inversion on F in combination with a prime form on E, he gets a chromatic hexachord from D to G. The hexachord of the original set runs from F to Bb. In this way, he achieves a new transposition level in a functional way.

What this gets us into is the question of what trichords have to do with hexachords and what hexachords have to do with the world. And this opens a whole different line of inquiry, which actually is a confluence of what Webern did and what Schoenberg did. I am speaking of the ways you can project sets and set lines, maintaining the original ordering by register, by meter, by various other "nominal" dimensions of the piece. We're accustomed to doing it with instruments. In the Webern, however, we're doing it with metrical placement. It can also be done with dynamics or with rhythmic differentiation. The opening trichord of the inversion on F could have been embedded in a hexachord of a different structure. But would it have been possible to begin another set form on some pitch class other than E and still get a chromatic hexachord? Let's do a little speculative composition here and see what would happen. Suppose, for example, that Webern had continued the following way.

EXAMPLE 2-13

Now obviously what we said before is no longer true—no longer do we have a chromatic hexachord. Could he have chosen another interval of imitation? Think about it for a second. Use manuscript paper; use your ears; use anything that seems musically pertinent, reasonable, available. It's worth thinking about because it takes one into completely different sets of considerations about hexachords, and about trichord relations.

Never think of these things as some sort of mechanistic way of going about writing a piece. They have to do with certain properties that are built into the whole notion of ordering hierarchization. They apply to any kind of serial music including non-twelve-tone serial music. (You can see this doesn't necessarily involve twelve tones; this is hexachordal composition, if you wish, which many people still indulge in.) The properties are obviously generalizations which can be interpreted in, quite literally, infinitely many different ways. Musically, they are not necessarily determining the foreground of your piece. They are determining it in the Webern *Symphony*, but, after all, that is a very early piece, and it was, to my knowledge, the first time such a thing was ever done. Schoenberg did something like it in the *Ode to Napoleon*, which was later, but obviously neither was going to conjoin fully his technique with the other's, because each of these people was maintaining his own particular position.

This brings us to the more general subject of what a trichord can generate by way of a hexachord. Well, what a trichord can generate by way of a hexachord is very constrained. It's not as if it can just project anything in the world, or that I can start anywhere and get just anything. We already saw in the horn variation how Webern generated a chromatic hexachord from two inversionally related forms of 013. Let's see if we can generate a different type of hexachord from 013. If we transpose the line of the canon that begins on E by a tritone, we get the situation shown in example 2-13. Notice that the hexachord now is 023457, and that we've made it harder for the horn player. Of course, we could have accomplished the same conjunction of trichords simply by having employed the retrograde of the set which we transposed. These hexachords—012345 and 023457—are the only two all-combinatorial hexachords that could be so arrived at, believe it or not. I could give you other lovely hexachords, but you could never generate them from this trichord under any conditions.

But now I would like to look at two kinds of generalizations regarding Schoenberg's use of hexachords. For one of these generalizations, I have to keep coming back to *Jakobsleiter* because there's no other comparable example in the literature. *Jakobsleiter* has the famous hexachord, the kind of hexachord other than the kind that Schoenberg virtually always used. Schoenberg's usual hexachord gives you the possibility of combination with a transposed inversion of itself to yield an aggregate. But the *Jakobsleiter* hexachord and its complement are not inversionally related to one another; rather, they're internally inversional. That is, the *Jakobsleiter* hexachord can invert into itself.

EXAMPLE 2-14

For Schoenberg, as I have already mentioned (see Chapter 1), the use of this hexachord seemed to be absolutely impossible. He tried and, as far as he was concerned, he failed. Like this hexachord, the hexachords he normally used had combinatorial properties, but their combinatoriality was of a different kind. If you try to find hexachords that are both self-inversional and inversionally related to their complements, you're bound to get hexachords with other properties as well—hexachords that also create aggregates with themselves under transposition. If you wanted to create an internally inversional hexachord like the *Jakobsleiter* hexachord which is related to its complement only by transposition, you couldn't do it. There's only one hexachord in the world that is transpositionally related to its complement but not also inversionally related to its complement. This is a form of it.

EXAMPLE 2-15

Notice the characteristic of this is that if I transpose it at the tritone, it yields an aggregate by transposition—perfectly obvious, the reason being there are no tritones here. There are other hexachords that have no tritones, but they would yield other things. I tell you this only because there is no way you can get another one that just has this property without having Schoenbergian properties, too. This is so deep and so complicated, there's no reason to waste any time on it. I mean theoretically deep, because it's not going to affect your compositional life. It's the kind of issue that tells you something about the chromatic structure, but it's not going to have any effect upon any uses of this hexachord or any analysis of this piece. It just happens to be an unexpected result of the relationships among hexachords.

Hexachords, as you know, are very fancy creatures. But the generalization which I've now confronted you with regarding all-combinatorial hexachords is something which I promise you I would not offer if we were just dealing with the question of kinds of hexachords. If this were just a matter of things that happen locally and make various combinations and create aggregates and do rather fancy things of that local kind, that would be interesting, but really nothing so important that it has to be regarded as anything more than the technique of a few composers. But it's much more than that. No matter what you do, if you work with trichords, if you work with any kind of contrapuntal ideas, you end up with these things manifesting themselves either on the surface or below the surface.

Let's look at the six all-combinatorial hexachords in normal form because there's a strange hierarchical relationship among them. First, there is the chromatic hexachord which Webern used constantly but never to create aggregates.

Hexachord #1

EXAMPLE 2-16a

There is the next one, next in one of the many ways of conceiving of these, that is, thinking about the circle-of-fifths aspect.

Hexachord #2

EXAMPLE 2-16b

Then, the next one in the same sense.

Hexachord #3

EXAMPLE 2-16c

These are the only three first-order sets, that is to say, those which will combine with themselves to create aggregates with every possible transformation at one and only one transpositional interval.

These three hexachords are related to each other in a sense similar to diatonic collections on the circle of fifths. Suppose you thought of the circle of fifths as being generated by simply changing one note. Suppose, for example, you thought of going from C to G by a very simple process of changing a semitone F to F♯. We are now dealing with the relation between the chromatic system and the circle-of-fifths system. Suppose I should say to you, all that I have to do to get the second hexachord from the first or the third from the second is exactly the same kind of operation. If I transposed C♯ in the first hexachord by a tritone, I'd get G and thus the second hexachord. And if I transposed D♯ in the second hexachord by a tritone, I'd get A and thus the third hexachord. Symmetrically, if you transpose the E of the second hexachord by a tritone, you get B♭ C D E♭ F G, which is also a transposition of the third hexachord. One-note difference, by the tritone. It's a tritone system. Exactly like the circle of fifths, we go right through them.

You might say, "What's the point of deriving these hexachords from each other?" Let me begin to answer that by saying some rather general musical things. There was a period of "composing with the tones of a motive" when composers were working with what they called "tonic sonorities." This term, frequent in the literature of the period, is used to refer to an arbitrary collection of pitches which is acted upon so as to generate a piece. These composers were first of all working in the spirit of minimum mutilation—a notion coming out of tonal music, where you're basically stuck with the same structures: you changed their function, you changed the "tonic" or the centricity. Now how about music in which you change the actual structure of the referential sonority? There was a great deal of such music in the twenties, and some of it incorporated this idea within pieces that operated on much larger principles. This is of course one way of viewing the hexachords. What you're doing when you derive one from another is changing the structure of your referential hexachord.

But there are many other ways to get from one to another. There's another way of viewing the whole thing. Suppose you think of the first hexachord as being constructed of two whole-tone trichords superposed.

EXAMPLE 2-17a

Then move one of the trichords up by a whole tone: you've got the next.

EXAMPLE 2-17b

You can think of it as sliding whole tones: if you slide one more step, you get the third hexachord.

EXAMPLE 2-17c

Half-whole-tone scales and whole-tone scales play a big role in all this. They are the underlying divisor, and we're talking about symmetries all the time. To repeat, you take the C E D and the C♯ D♯ E♯; you move the C♯ D♯ E♯ by one whole tone and you've transposed it onto a part of itself—that old Webernian compositional technique (although we're not really talking about compositional techniques here). Then we take D♯ F G and move it up one whole step, and we get the third hexachord. And that's just another way of viewing it. So you've got a path just like the circle of fifths except you're changing intervallic structures rather than changing transposition levels, but the structures share a very fundamental characteristic: they all are all-combinatorial.

Now we're dealing with this abstractly, but all of these relationships are bound to manifest themselves compositionally when these hexachords are used. Now notice another important relationship: the first and third hexachords are both generable by a single interval. The first is a chromatic scale, generable by a semitone. The third is a circle of fifths generated by a fifth; it is nothing more, as you can see, than a major scale minus one tone. So therefore the circle-of-fifths transform—M5, so-called—will generate the first hexachord from the third and vice versa. The idea of a circle-of-fifths transform has its historical origins in Bartok; it is a remarkable example of a transformation that looks extremely artificial because it changes quantitative relations—sizes—and yet maintains every conceivable structural relation. Hexachords, trichords, their relationship—it maintains a whole cosmos of relationships. Some of this is in my article "Since Schoenberg."[2] Do you all know what I mean by a circle-of-fifths transform? If you multiply each of the intervals in the first hexachord by five, mod 12, which is exactly the same thing as mapping the chromatic scale onto the circle of fifths or vice versa—it's a symmetrical operation—you get the third hexachord. If you apply the same operation, to the second hexachord, what do you think you'll get? You get the same hexachord again. So the second hexachord is structurally very, very different from the other two. You cannot generate it by a single interval.

Now, before we complete this survey, let me show you one more intuitively unexpected and non obvious set of tensions. Notice that in these hexachords you have every possible interval except for one: the tritone. And it's this tritone, of course, which we were using as the basis of transposition. It's the boundary interval, the one missing interval. We know from our general principles of both index numbers and transpositions that if we transpose any of these hexachords by a tritone (the interval they lack), then the resultant will have no notes in common, and therefore we will get an aggregate.

Writing an all-interval set is one of the things that concerned many, many composers early in the game—and still does, because it has very valuable properties if you're going to write a certain kind of piece. Writing an all-interval set with one of these first-order all-combinatorial hexachords is very hard to do, because of the problem of meeting two different groups of constraints. There's basically only one all-interval set associated with each hexachord. That may not be obvious, but it's not unexpected. But on the other hand, other things *are* unexpected.

Now, remember what goes on with the Schoenberg aggregate. You have a set. You can combine it with one particular inversion, with one particular retrograde, with one particular retrograde inversion maintaining respective hexachordal collections. The retrograde is a trivial one, of course, and the retrograde inversion simply has the same relation to the inversion that the retrograde has to the prime. You thus have four sets which together constituted for Schoenberg an area—an area which maintained hexachord collections. There are thus twelve distinct areas, each containing four sets. (In fact, the Fourth Quartet also goes beyond hexachords, to tetrachords and trichords.)

Now the idea of twelve areas obviously appealed to Schoenberg; the analogy with twelve pitch classes was a very important one for him, both from the standpoint of a circle of fifths as well as from the standpoint of his series of twelve tones. In the Suite, Opus 29, Schoenberg worked with a third-order all-combinatorial set but he didn't treat it as such. He treated it as if it were just any other inversionally combinatorial set. This leads to some pretty funny things because there are places where he thinks he is landing in a new area, but from a combinatorial point of view, it's the same hexachord.

Schoenberg laid these things out by just writing down every single one of the twenty-four forms of the series (he was willing to read the retrogrades from right to left). And he wrote it all out in pitch-class notation, not in numerical notation. After writing down all the set forms, he would write down what the distance was between the transpositions—plus one, minus one, plus two, minus two, and so on. The unity of all this evaded him completely because he had no unified notion of it: there was none at that time. For him, the four combinatorially related set forms constituted a tonic area, so to speak, and I'm sure that analogy played a much larger role in his thinking than he allowed anybody to know. But with hexachord #1 you have a set combinable with a form of itself under transposition (by interval 6). And so for all the other first-order hexachords. The first-order hexachords thus double the number of sets contained in a family of sets which define an area. As a result, first-order hexachords have six areas, each containing eight sets.

And now, let's complete our discussion of the all-combinatorial hexachords. You see, there seems to be a leap now. The fourth hexachord is a second-order hexachord, and you can see why it would be so.

Hexachord #4

EXAMPLE 2-18a

There are missing intervals of 3 and 9. And therefore if we transpose it to 3 or to 9, we will get aggregates. This hexachord—a second-order set—has only three areas: those defined by itself and two transpositions. Each of these areas contains sixteen sets. The greater the degree of combinatoriality, of course, the fewer the number of contrasting structural, "functional" areas. That's bound to have its effect, too, of course: an immediate compositional effect.

This second-order hexachord, for example, has a matching of tritones (C–F♯, C♯–G, and D–A♭). That means when you have any kind of contrapuntal combination, you're going to have a repetition of intervals because, of course, they will occur in association with tritones; and as we've seen, this does not apply only to note-against-note counterpoint. This property gives no particular priority to note-against-note, because you're going to get these constancies no matter how you line up the notes, as long as you do it with contextual consistency.

You can work these through hierarchically. Hexachord #5 has three boundary intervals, that is to say, three missing intervals: 2, 6, and 10.

Hexachord #5

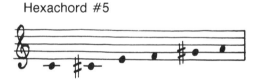

EXAMPLE 2-18b

That reduces the number of areas to two. And then, of course, hexachord #6 is there for the Frenchmen.

Hexachord #6

EXAMPLE 2-18c

It is the whole-tone scale, which, of course, has only one area: the one defined by itself and its complement. The boundary intervals—the missing intervals—are every odd interval: 1, 3, 5, 7, etc.

Now that's all there is and all there has to be.

These six hexachords have a significance far beyond their local occurrences in pieces. No matter what you work with—trichords, tetrachords, or what-not—they end up being not only classifiable in these terms but also projecting one of these hexachords. The all-combinatorial hexachords will be the under-lying structures in a piece whether or not you begin with them explicitly.

Take a particular ordering of hexachord #4, and combine it with one of the two inversions that will yield an aggregate.

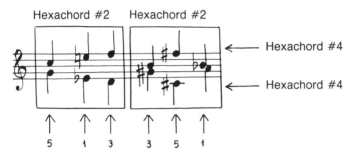

EXAMPLE 2-19

I'm sticking with inversion here although, heaven knows, I don't have to. I think you can see that I'm not cheating you or doing anything vulgar. Notice that the first three intervals (5, 1, and 3) come again in the second half of example 2-19, although not in the same order. I'm simply running a particular ordering of this hexachord against an inversion of itself. Notice that each collection of three simultaneous dyads is a transposition of hexachord #2. This is bound to happen. You can't avoid it. I'm writing it note-against-note for simplicity's sake, but the collection will still be the same, no matter how we order them in time. The point of all this is that these different all-combinatorial hexachords are interrelated again at more foreground levels. There's nothing in the world to suggest to you that there's an inherent rela-tionship between hexachord #4 and hexachord #2, and, as a matter of fact, there is no way of getting from one to the other hierarchically that would seem simple and logical as part of the larger pattern. It would just have to come out in the musical surface depending on the extent to which you want to use one hexachord to then go into another region and into another structure. Obviously we're now getting into decisions that would be made within a composition.

Now I want to look at the way in which one could arrive at a Schoenbergian combinatorial hexachord by a simple method involving index numbers. I want to demonstrate to you that index numbers are not just an analogy, not just an analog—in the inversional domain—of interval in the transpositional domain. Suppose you want to create a Schoenbergian hexachord, that is, one which combines with itself under inversion to create an aggregate. Suppose we start with the note C; and I say, "All right, I'm going to create a Schoenbergian aggregate, or a Schoenbergian hexachord which will create an aggregate." I'm just going to start from scratch: with my C in the first hexachord, give me a corresponding note in the complementary hexachord. Just give me an arbitrary note.

ANSWER: F.

Good man. You didn't fall into my trap (ex. 2-20a).

EXAMPLE 2-20a

But if you were just doing this in a random fashion, you could have been stuck with the very first note you chose. It might not have been possible to have a Schoenbergian hexachord. That tells you something about the constraints of the property, the constraints on the choice. If you had said, for example, A♭, it would not have worked. It would be absolutely impossible for this to be a set in which these two hexachords would be inversions of one another and, therefore, Schoenbergian. If for any pitch-class X in the first hexachord, you choose a corresponding pitch-class Y in the second—which of course is going to be a transposed inversion of the first—then X plus Y is going to be an index number. But if the index number you start with is even, you are stuck. You won't be able to complete the set. Let's see why. With a

0 in the first hexachord and an 8 in the second, some time you're going to have a 4 in one of the hexachords and you're also going to need a 4 in the other and you're stuck. Forget the arithmetic! There's nothing esoteric about the mathematics. What is important is to realize that already certain kinds of intervallic relationships, if you wish, pitch relationships, are absolutely impossible within the Schoenbergian domain.

On the other hand, his hexachords are by no means rare. It is simple to create one of these! Let's go back to the F. If we have a C (0) in one hexachord and F (5) in the other, then the rest follows easily. If I put, say, a B (11) next to the C, that means that I have to have an F♯ (6) in the other hexachord.

EXAMPLE 2-20b

And so it will go because the index number has to remain fixed. Once we have an odd index number, for any note you give me I can always find a partner. A G in the first hexachord will require a B♭ in the second.

EXAMPLE 2-20c

I'm making this seem even more trivial than it is, and remember, we haven't ordered these hexachords. If I had written down pitch-class numbers instead of notes, then intuitively it wouldn't have been so obvious. To finish this up, a 4 in the first hexachord will give us a 1 in the second. 2 and 3 will go together although it doesn't matter which hexachord each is in as long as they are in different ones, so this leaves us with only the pair of pitches left. If you have an 8 you must have 9, but regarding which hexachord each goes in, you're a master of your fate.

EXAMPLE 2-20d

All this has resulted in a collection which is not obvious by any means. That is, its relationship to its complement is not at all obvious when you look at it this way. We might retain this ordering, particularly if you like minor triads and things like that—if you're a traditionalist. We can also change the ordering, and get something quite different. I could, for example, give you a trichord that we didn't have in our first version, putting the 9, 10, and 6 next to each other. I hope you don't think anybody writes music this way (although maybe somebody does). From the standpoint of ordering, this is a very different hexachord from the earlier one. Basically what we have through this entire discussion is a tiny little formula which says X plus Y equals some index number where X is in the first hexachord, Y is in the second. That's all we have been doing. In this way, you can begin to create a unified theory of all of this.

Suppose now we took the same formula giving you an index number, but with the related pitches in the *same* hexachord. That gives you the *Jakobsleiter* hexachord, the one which is its own inversion. Therefore, both the hexachord and its complement are their own inversions independently, and they can be very different. In this case, if I choose some first note, any second note for the same hexachord will be possible. Now nothing is impossible. The process of building the hexachord note by note may tell you something about Schoenberg's problem with this kind of a hexachord. It does not have the same kind of constraints as the hexachords we discussed earlier. Of course, you can get the same number of aggregates with this kind of a hexachord as you can with those that invert into their complements. But, more deeply, the constraints are obviously different, because, for example, I'm not constrained with regard to whatever second note I choose. In other words, I'll take that A♭ that I couldn't take before. That says I've got a 0 and an 8, so if I want a 4, I get a 4. And if I want to kill that augmented triad a little bit, if I have this 3, I simply stick in a 5, but, of course, now I have to choose a 10, because 10 plus 10 gives me an 8. And now I have it.

EXAMPLE 2-21

I have an internally inversionally symmetrical hexachord, not unlike the chord from Schoenberg's Opus 16, Number 3. In other words, we can invert this into itself with an index number of 8, giving us Ab, C, E, F, Eb, Bb. Of course, the second hexachord can be wildly different as a result. The little tiny detail that we just saw about no restriction on the choice of the second note might tell you something about the difference in the constraints.

Now I've got something terrible to tell you. We haven't done anything about those relationships which are supposed to be operations on order: retrogrades and retrograde inversions. We've worked only with inversion because we have so many direct examples in the literature and because time is short. Actually the retrograde and the retrograde inversion also have exactly such constancies, although their constancies are a little more removed. But for all the things we've done with inversion (and there are many, many hundreds more, some of which are in various articles), retrograde and the retrograde inversion similarly show a tremendous amount about the unification of inter-vallic relationships within the system. Let me just show you. Let's take the set from Schoenberg's Fourth Quartet again, although it makes no difference— all of these things by their very nature are true for any sets anywhere, at any time, without regard to hexachordal structure, or race or creed. I'm going to write out an arbitrary retrograde inversion, not a combinatorial one or any like that, just an absolutely arbitrary one.

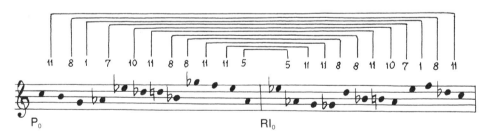

EXAMPLE 2-22

Look what happens. The intervals of the set repeat in reverse order. That's the remarkable thing about the retrograde inversion: it's an intervallic constancy—it just repeats the interval. That's the reason that Schoenberg usually uses it first, because he's going to get intervals in common.

Now I'm going to write a set note-against-note above its retrograde inversion in order to show an interesting constant aspect.

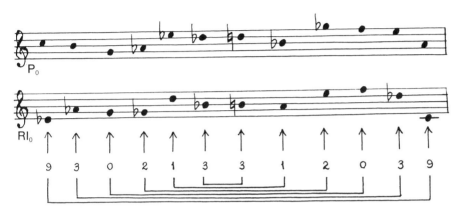

EXAMPLE 2-23

I'm not going to apologize for writing note-against-note anymore, because you know this is just a model and you can temporally expand from that in any direction that you wish. I'm also not going to apologize for writing these things in time, because you know I could easily be writing the same things in space. I'm purposely not getting any aggregates, although I could have done so. Now, do you see anything happening that looks like what happens with inversion, any constancies or repetitions, or patterns, that recur? The relations that result from conjoining inversionally related sets are not obvious to many people at first because they depend on the structure of the set and on what transpositional interval you use. But certain things are bound to maintain: repetition of pitch dyads, repetition of interval dyads between elements a tritone apart, etc. Now what would you expect of the retrograde inversion which is so close to home? It's exactly like the inversion except it is now temporally reversed. The dyadic intervals in the first half of example 2-23 are the same as in the second half but in reverse order.

The retrograde, believe it or not, is more complex. What would you expect with retrograde comparably? What we're getting at is a kind of unification. Remember, the retrograde inversion basically sets up an intervallic repetition, which you'd expect because the intervals repeat. Now what would the retrograde do? It's a little harder to intuit: running a retrograde against a prime will give you a succession of index numbers exactly the same as the succession of interval numbers you get when you run a retrograde inversion against a prime.

P_0:	0	11	7	8	3	1	2	10	6	5	4	9
R_0:	9	4	5	6	10	2	1	3	8	7	11	0
Index:	9	3	0	2	1	3	3	1	2	0	3	9

EXAMPLE 2-24

Similarly, the index numbers formed by the combination of prime and retrograde inversion will correspond to the intervals formed between prime and retrograde.

P_0:	0	11	7	8	3	1	2	10	6	5	4	9
RI_0:	3	8	7	6	2	10	11	9	4	5	1	0
Index:	3	7	2	2	5	11	1	7	10	10	5	9

P_0:	0	11	7	8	3	1	2	10	6	5	4	9
R_0:	9	4	5	6	10	2	1	3	8	7	11	0
Interval:	3	7	2	2	5	11	1	7	10	10	5	9

EXAMPLE 2-25

COMMENT: On a 12 × 12, the diagonal that goes in the wrong direction defines the same succession.

Absolutely. That's exactly right. It's very easy to see that on the 12 × 12 matrix.

0	11	7	8	3	1	2	10	6	5	4	9
1	0	8	9	4	2	3	11	7	6	5	10
5	4	0	1	8	6	7	3	11	10	9	2
4	3	11	0	7	5	6	2	10	9	8	1
9	8	4	5	0	10	11	7	3	2	1	6
11	10	6	7	2	0	1	9	5	4	3	8
10	9	5	6	1	11	0	8	4	3	2	7
2	1	9	10	5	3	4	0	8	7	6	11
6	5	1	2	9	7	8	4	0	11	10	3
7	6	2	3	10	8	9	5	1	0	11	4
8	7	3	4	11	9	10	6	2	1	0	5
3	2	10	11	6	4	5	1	9	8	7	0

EXAMPLE 2-26

And so we begin to go. These things I've told you indicate something about the interrelationships of intervallic content and intervallic ordering and their very strange kinds of constraints.

3 Large-Scale Harmonic Organization

The relation of the harmonic and the contrapuntal in twelve-tone serialism really depends upon the way in which certain kinds of linear things conjoin to create complexes—only partially ordered complexes—which turn out to be related to extensions of those linear things themselves. Now the obvious example of this (one that's now become very familiar to you) is the opening of the Schoenberg Fourth Quartet. Much of this is also true of the Schoenberg Violin Concerto and, in a more complex way, the Schoenberg Trio. Let's go back to the Fourth Quartet for a moment and use it as a basis for recalling some general principles. Doing so will carry us into the whole issue of counterpoint and harmony: how quite disparate elements, when treated similarly, somehow can turn out to be inherently conjoinable because of what they generate in common.

I'm going back to the Fourth Quartet because I want to justify a fairly pretentious statement that I'm given to making about the construal of such pieces which I hope I can instance fairly simply in this piece. I hope you don't think that the only piece that exemplifies these things is the Fourth Quartet, but I am using it for a number of reasons. It is a quartet and is therefore easier to deal with as a medium than the Violin Concerto. You can't look at even the beginning of the Violin Concerto without looking at the instrumentation (like the things that go on in the lines of the celli), and if you start writing those down, you end up virtually reproducing the entire score. It's just a matter of practicality. I will talk a little bit about Schoenberg's Opus 33a later and, above all, *Moses and Aaron*. The *Moses and Aaron* problem is very severe because of the complexity of the score, but that's one that I don't feel

I can afford to skip. At the beginning of pieces such as these, there's already such a reach of reference, such a scope of relatedness, that it is crucial to hear it accurately.

Whether such construal is possible is, no doubt, a question that has to be decided taking into account the time the passage occupies, the amount of time you have to take it in, and how it carries you through the time. Then there is the question of so-called directed motion. You have every reason to ask what directs it, what kind of motion? But if you want to use the term with regard to tonal music, I think you can use it analogously with regard to the Fourth Quartet. When you reach a certain point in this piece, you recognize the fact that what is happening has been adumbrated, that it has been implied by secondary aspects of earlier parts of the piece. Let me try to justify this.

The obvious characteristic of this piece, which is to be found in any book, is the very explicit initial statement of the series, or set (with all of the registral characteristics that I have spoken about elsewhere). It is important to realize that, when you've heard the second hexachord, you already know things that are going to happen in a very different kind of situation. They're going to happen contrapuntally; they're going to suggest the total movement of the piece; but more of that in a moment.

Let's look at the opening measures. In the first five beats you have one of these things that people regard as counting up to twelve and everybody's happy and we can proceed. It is certainly true that this all adds up to an aggregate. I'm using the word *aggregate* because there's absolutely no basis whatsoever for regarding this as totally ordered, even after you've heard the piece and you might begin to infer dispositionally what the series of the piece can be inferred to be. There is no reason to assume that within these simultaneities one of these notes precedes another, unless spatial and temporal ordering are being preserved, which they're not here. There are other criteria at work for the spatial and the instrumental dispositions and assignments. The obvious thing that everyone talks about is that the first chord has the same content as the second three notes in the first violin, the second chord corresponds to its third linear trichord, and the third chord to its fourth linear trichord. That's certainly true, and it certainly gives you an aggregate. But of course, one has a perfect right to ask (if one wants music to be as much as it can be) why the notes are assigned as they are. There is no direct kind of correlation here. The registral order of the first chord (F, E♭, B♭) does not, for

EXAMPLE 3-1

example, suggest the disposition in space of the equivalent trichord in the first violin, which would be some composers' approach. It would work if the Bb were an octave lower and the F an octave higher, but Schoenberg doesn't do that. Nor does he do it with the other trichords.

What is interesting is that certain notes in the first violin are attacked simultaneously with certain chords. Now all of these things together begin to suggest that you'd better listen to register; you'd better listen to instrument. The hexachord C#–D–F#–Ab–A–Bb is registrally and instrumentally homogenous; both instruments playing it are violins; things are kept very clean. And the hexachord in the viola and cello, C–B–G–F–E–D#—the remaining six pitch classes—is the transposed inversion of the higher one. This is familiar, I know, to most of us. If we look at this more closely, we realize why these assignments have been made. If you listen to this as it proceeds, retrospectively perhaps, you'll recognize the fact that the six notes in the viola and cello are a transposition of the first six notes in the first violin, and therefore the first six notes in the violins are a transposition of the last six notes of the first violin.

EXAMPLE 3-2

In other words, what he's building into this piece (what he's, if you wish, burying under its surface, though it's not very deeply buried) is a basis for transposition of his two hexachords. And the two hexachords are inversions of one another. So in a sense, he is simply replicating his hexachords in the harmonic and contrapuntal structures. Now the way that becomes the beginning of a path is what I want to talk about. This is something I could document with regard to the exact points where this path is articulated in the piece. But for now I'd rather give you the general idea.

The first six pitch classes in the violins are these, written in a kind of ascending normal form.

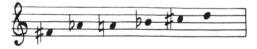

EXAMPLE 3-3

What you get very much accustomed to hearing in this piece is this collection of pitches, a very clear division of the chromatic with pitch classes in a characteristic arrangement in clusters of two semitones and one semitone and a single isolated note. Notice again that the second hexachord in the first violin is a transposition of it. It may seem to be belaboring the obvious (but it never seems to have been that obvious) that what you're getting here, by virtue of a choice that obviously was deliberately made involving these notes, the intervallic relations of which had to be built into the structure of this set, is a region defined by the instrumentation that is exactly the same as the region defined by the successive hexachords of the first violin by itself. The second region is a major second away.

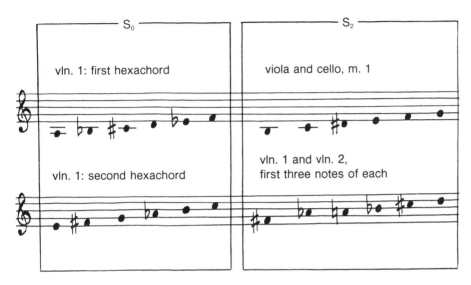

EXAMPLE 3-4

And then, of course, the hexachord in the viola and cello therefore has to be a transposition of the first hexachord of the first violin. The second region is thus S_2 with regard to S_0. I would not deny that, primarily, you're going to hear the line that the first violin plays accompanied by the chords played by the others. You're also going to hear these chords associating registrally. It's very hard to hear on the records, but very easy to hear in a room, and, of course, a lot will be up to the quartet. Further, no one would say for a moment that if you don't hear this the first time, the piece falls apart. Of course not. What is important, however, is that you're going to arrive eventually at the region in which this S_2 is the primary form of the set. And when you get there, you're going to hear the pitches of the hexachord of S_2 associated in such a way that there will be absolutely no doubt in your mind that somehow, somewhere, each group of six has been associated before. So when we reach this point (m. 120), this S_2, we've gotten to a point in the piece that has been adumbrated in the opening.

This, then, is one instance of what I mean by a contextual path through the piece, a path that is dependent upon the structure of this particular series and, indeed, the ordering of this particular series. This is a point that may not seem particularly clear, because you might say, "Well, you're simply dealing with collections of notes; the ordering doesn't seem to be consequential." Of course, that's not true. The relationship between ordering and collection is absolutely crucial to Schoenberg and most other twelve-tone composers. What seemed suddenly to vivify for Schoenberg the whole notion of how this total ordering of the twelve pitch classes could be employed was this idea of maintaining a collection within the ordering, this interplay, this change of hierarchization between the role of ordering and the role of collection. It may seem I'm only talking about collections when I say that the first six notes of the first violin are the same as the first six notes of the viola and cello together, to within transposition. You might ask what this has to do with ordering. But please remember that if he hadn't ordered the trichords as he did, he could not have gotten the collection combinations to the degree of accuracy necessary: he needed at least the B♭ in the second trichord, the A♭ in the third, etc. This may seem complex to some of you—either one knows this stuff very well or it seems very remote—but I want to emphasize the essential musical point: what you have here is a basis for moving through a piece, a basis defined by the set and not by any principles shared by any other piece. In this is the particular richness and strength of this piece, and the particular difficulties of pieces like this.

Let me show you why and how Schoenberg has built into the structure of this set a uniqueness of ordering for every given segment of this set. Schoenberg has arranged things so that if we combine the first hexachord with a transposition of its inversion, we get our familiar aggregate. If you think the word *aggregate* is occurring too frequently in this discussion, and that I'm flogging some kind of a horse, the answer is that you can't talk about Schoenberg and a lot of other composers without it, because it represents the first stage in which an ordering relationship is (I don't want to say weakened) altered by virtue of retaining the ordered segments and combining them to create a collection which replicates the total chromatic of the set itself. This creates the possibility, without violating any of the component orderings, of new foreground orderings and of moving you one step forward in the structure of the piece. This is the familiar hexachordal combinatoriality.

If you look at this set, you'll also notice something about the ordering of the tetrachords. You don't usually talk about tetrachords with Schoenberg, but all of these things function in this particular set and in most of his sets.

As with the hexachords, he wanted a hierarchization among tetrachords. To achieve this, he chose the only inversional transpositional relationship which will yield this particular reflection of the total chromatic. (This may be unfamiliar to some of you. Either it's one of those things that's your native language or it's not. But you should never be intimidated by numbers of any kind.) If you look at the tetrachords, you'll notice something about them.

EXAMPLE 3-5

The second and third tetrachords are the same type from any reasonable collectional point of view; therefore structurally, unordered, we'll say they're the same. Anything that's true of a collection is true of any ordering of that collection. Of course, the reverse is by no means true. The first tetrachord is unto itself. Look at it for a moment and you'll see that it's internally inversionally equivalent to itself. That is, you can map it into itself under inversion. Notice that the second and third tetrachords are inversionally equivalent to each other. That means that under some inversional value, when I map the total set into its own inversion, I'm going to get a replication of the first tetrachord, and the second and third are going to map into each other. I want to get these things clearly in your minds so that you can see this sort of systematic linkage.

Let me just for a moment show you what will happen if I invert the set starting on 7. The first tetrachord maps into itself as a collection, while the second maps into the third and vice versa.

S_0 (D = 0)

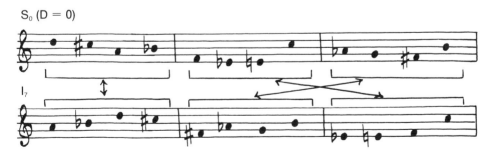

EXAMPLE 3-6

That simply means that I_7 involves a distinguished, unique preservation of tetrachords. When Schoenberg reaches I_7, he has an association with his original statement of the set that cannot be reached at any other level of inversion or in any other transformation. So S_0 is associated with I_7 in this way.

This goes one step farther, as you'll see if you consider the trichords.

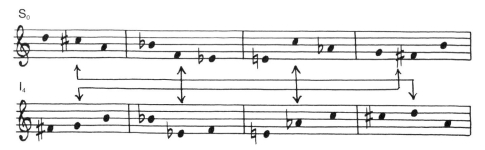

EXAMPLE 3-7

The tetrachords cut across the trichords, so in order to preserve the property we just mentioned, the B♭ had to be the first element of the second trichord. There's thus a high degree of determinacy in all of this, once you conjoin and combine all of these characteristics. As for the trichords themselves, the first trichord and the last trichord are the same type. The second trichord is internally symmetrical, as is the third (the augmented triad). So all you have to do is choose I_4. Then, of course, the last trichord is going to map into the first one and vice versa; in each of these there is a duplication of content with a change of order in the first two elements. The second and third trichords map into each other with a change in order in the last two elements. The changes in order that such transformations induce are fundamental to the way the piece goes. These are constantly being exploited. There are all kinds of symmetries and associations. Virtually no change can be made in this kind of set structure without altering the fundamental aspects of these associations.

Now let me go back to where we were with the hexachordal regions. How Schoenberg reaches the S_2 region is, of course, a matter of local techniques and all kinds of motivic things. It's an extremely complicated piece of course. But when we reach S_2 (and this is really the crux of what I have to say about this piece), what do we have? S_2 has no associations with regard to retentions of components of the set but is reached because of what is intimated by the first measure of the piece. The set associated hexachordally with the S_2 region is I_7, however, and I_7 does have a particular relationship to the original: it's the one that preserves the tetrachords (see ex. 3-6). S_2 brings with it I_7 (by hexachordal combinatoriality), but S_2 can also be associated with I_9, which preserves its tetrachords, and with I_6, which preserves its trichords. So you see how the chain begins to move. Each stage involves a collection of pitch statements, or set statements or series statements, each having its own internal associations and referring back to some particular striking characteristic of the point from which you have come.

This chain of relationships is based upon a number of different criteria. The first is the way the instrumentation was set up at the beginning. That, of course, was done as a thematic element. The rest are built into the structure of the set. After all, you could have associated S_2 with this I_7, which, in most cases and for most composers, would make all the aggregates you want but would have absolutely no relation to the original point from which you've come. But the reason Schoenberg builds S_2 into the instrumentation is because I_7, combinatorially related to S_2, also retains the tetrachords of S_0.

Now this can go on and on, by which I mean one can trace the path through here with all kinds of details. When he reaches S_2, he already begins to prepare the next point. The thing about these opening chords, by the way, is that they have the same kind of relations to this piece as certain things do in Mozart and Beethoven. The opening chords, for example, never occur in the same way ever again. When you look at the score, you may be disappointed, because when you get a statement of the set on E (S_2), it's not laid out as it was in the opening. It's not going to be laid out for you ever again in the piece as it was then. That's, of course, one of the decisions a composer makes. How obvious, how explicit am I going to be? When he reaches S_2 things change but they're textural things. All kinds of associations are made dynamically; that is the nature of this piece and a few pieces of Schoenberg. Not many have this degree of complexity or intricacy, if you wish. When you reach that S_2 it's a well-defined change in the course of the piece. As we have seen, when he reaches the point where the set begins on E (S_2), the hexachordally combinatorial form will now be on A (I_7). Then we look and see that that's the one that, of course, preserves the tetrachords of the one on D (S_0). And he reflects all that in one way or another in the piece.

I'm not trying to sell you anything—I don't have to tell you that. I'm trying to explicate something. It's perfectly reasonable for a reasonably competent listener to say, "Look, how in the devil can I take this in?" I'm not going to respond to that question because what we've been discussing is there in the first measure, and you will certainly eventually hear it. It is not going to be as clear on the records as it would be, of course, live, or as I would like it to be.

There's a place in the piece where this theme is stated very high, transposed at the tritone. People who insist that music is satisfactory only if it has certain patterns of recurrence (which are called *form* in some circles) want to call that a recapitulation. Well, if you like recapitulations at the tritone without anything else being the same, call it a recapitulation, if it comforts you. But the truth of the matter is that this is very misleading because it's not so much a recapitulation as a simple thematic recall at the tritone. He's gotten to that particular transposition through a series of S_2's — S_2, S_4, S_6, and there you are. But the opening chords are not there. Instead he has the combinatorial inversion laid out against the theme to create aggregates, but partitioned in such a way that you'll also recall a lot of other things.

The notion of a composer trying at any moment of his piece to use any significant segment both to recall and to predict, to be retrospective and predictive, to tell you where you've been as well as where you're going to be, is, of course, to many composers, crucial. And either you run the risk of being too retrospective (which means too obvious), or you run the other risk of being too predictive (and therefore being opaque or perhaps losing a reasonable listener). I have to say *reasonable listener* although you know what kind of a cop-out that has to be. Stravinsky used the term *the hypothetical other;* of course, the hypothetical other is Stravinsky.[1] I know it's very hard to hear these things, but you would be amazed (and I could demonstrate this if we had a few months) at the extent to which you will hear these things and hear associations even though you would imagine it impossible to identify the things as things in themselves.

There's one aspect of this that we haven't talked about which just adds another level to the opening measures. Why does he state the second chord as a simultaneity with the C♯, while the other two chords are not attacked simultaneously with the attacks of the first violin? Can you see any reason why he'd want to make this delineation? It's the kind of thing that may seem like a tiny detail, but these are the tiny details that you may hear the fourth or fifth time. The second chord plus the C♯ replicates a segment of the set. The simultaneity with the C♯ is the same collection as, for example, E♭–E–C–A♭ and E–C–A♭–G within the set. Normally, Schoenberg would never put an augmented triad into a series. But here it is, with a semitone on each side of it. The simultaneity is thus a possible segment of a set form.

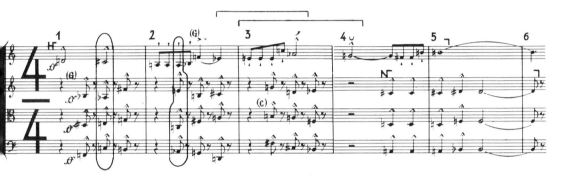

EXAMPLE 3-8

Notice also the similar sort of thing that happens in measure 2. According to Schoenberg's little pattern here, the first chord in measure 2 really belongs with the B♭ in the first violin, because the B♭ begins the second trichord of the set. Schoenberg puts the chord against the A instead, in order to get the same set type (an augmented triad plus a semitone) as the simultaneity we were discussing in measure 1. This is the kind of thing he does all the time. There are other simultaneities in this passage which also replicate segmental subsets of the series, but this one has more set resonances. It has more set implications and more immediate set implications. More than other sets here, this augmented-triad-plus-semitone has the additional ambiguity of being able to suggest multiple sets, and it accounts for many things in the second and fourth movements which are utterly incomprehensible otherwise. For example, you can easily see that C♯–C–A♭–E (the simultaneity in measure 1) could occur as a set segment in the inversion starting on D, but that's not the only form where it will occur.

The opening chords recur very early in the piece and in such a way as to delineate the end of the first section of the piece. Their rhythmic statement is such that it would be very hard to miss. It has always interested me perceptually or psychologically (whatever word you care to use) that they are often missed as restatements of these chords, though sonically and in every other respect they are the same chords. Beginning at the end of measure 15, he states the opening again, but this time purely as simultaneous tetrachords.

EXAMPLE 3-9

Now let's consider the chords beginning at the end of measure 16. You can't miss the sonorities—the E, F♯, B; the augmented triad (A, F, C♯); the B♭, D, D♯—the same trichords as the opening but at the combinatorial level (I_5).

Now go back and look at the comparable notes in the opening chords (m. 1): F, D♯, B♭; C, E, A♭; and B, G, F♯. The succession of chords beginning at the end of measure 16 is stated exactly as those in measure 1 were, but stated in such a way as to give you a sense of the inversion in the instrumental lines. The second violin in measure 1 has a line which goes down by a whole tone and up by a seventh. The first violin at the end of measure 16 (the comparable instrumental part) goes up by a whole tone and down by a seventh. The second violin and the viola at the end of measure 16 are similarly contour inversions of the viola and cello parts in measure 1. In other words, not only are the chords beginning at the end of measure 16 the inversion of the comparable chords in measure 1, but the inversion is one of linear contour as well.

Compare the chords beginning at the end of measure 15 with those beginning at the end of measure 16 for a similar kind of relationship. The trichord of the lower three parts of *A* (see ex. 3-9) is played in the three upper parts—chord *X*—at the end of measure 16. The trichord of the lower three parts of *B* becomes the trichord of the three parts in chord *Y*. Finally, the trichord in the bottom three parts in *C* becomes the trichord of the top three instruments on the second beat of measure 17—chord *Z*. Schoenberg keeps the lines of measure 1, and inverts these chords. Why do they recur in that way at those pitch levels? The only explanation involves combinatorial criteria. The criteria tell you a great deal about what constitutes an analogy or a repetition in this piece. The combinatorial inversion—that unique hexachord relationship—yields in all those comparable places those successions of notes. It is the determinant for relationships in all of these dimensions.

Let's change the subject. Schoenberg's Opus 33a begins so.

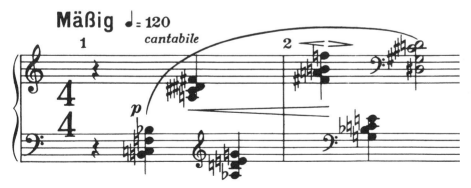

EXAMPLE 3-10

We're looking at something very different now, but which involves yet another way in which the relations on the surface reflect something much deeper in the piece. What I want to do here is just talk a little bit about one aspect. The piece begins with simply a series of three chords with four notes in each. This doesn't suggest necessarily a twelve-tone piece, except that the passage is chromatic and contains twelve different notes. The next thing you get is another four-note chord. Now, what would be the first association you'd be likely to make there? Well, I assume, if you've had any experience with the music, you would hear an immediate intervallic association even if you couldn't identify it. You hear the same intervals from bottom to top in the fourth chord that you heard from top to bottom in the third. That suggests already that there's some sort of familiar transformation going on, but you don't have to be able to identify the transformation to identify the fact that you're getting an altering of the interval order from top to bottom. That, obviously, is a repetition of some kind. And then the same thing happens again—the fifth chord is an inversion of the second. So you can pretty well guess what the next chord is going to be. The next chord is going to be D♯–G♯–C♯–D.

Of course you can do this with any twelve-tone collection in the world. But I'm trying to suggest that the ordering is of particular significance for this piece. The fact that he states the set in this, if you wish, arbitrary way—arbitrary in the sense that you can state any set this way—suggests that something else might be going on. The tetrachords don't have any particular kind of structural relation to each other; their relationships are absolutely systematic. The retrograde inversion simply reiterates the intervals of the original statement, so you're bound to get intervallic return, intervallic repetition. But what he's doing on the very foreground of the opening of the piece is telling you something very specific about the structure of the piece.

Why does he begin the second group of chords at that pitch level? He could have stated the retrograde inversion at any transposition level, and the intervallic repetition would still be there. So why did Schoenberg start on F? That is very tricky. This is a very different situation from the Fourth Quartet. The Opus 33a is a slightly earlier piece, but that's not the point. These pieces are very different for all that they do both employ certain basic principles of combination. I have no idea when I hear this piece how the notes of each chord are themselves ordered. I might have begun by looking at it as a succession of three internally unordered chords followed by a similar succession of three such chords, but that view would not reflect the associations between the internal orderings of each pair of chords. When I begin with the Bb in the first chord (just take the Bb because it's the uppermost note), the corresponding note, from the point of view of the contextual relations, is the D♯ in the sixth chord. The next note in the first chord is an F. The corresponding note in the sixth chord seems to be a G♯.

What's going on here is that he's telling you, in this direct, explicit foreground statement, something about the deep structure of this piece in terms of the relationships between his combinatorial hexachords. This initial statement is already beginning to tell you something although you can't quite infer yet what it is. This is a very different kind of relationship from the one you had in the Fourth Quartet. The essential question in Opus 33a is how you regard these two sets when they're taken in dyads and when those dyads are regarded as making tetrachords, not linearly but in groups of twos.

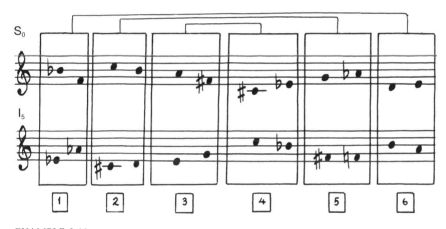

EXAMPLE 3-11

Now for those people who have had some experience with this, you'll already begin to recognize that something very special is happening in the piece. He has three tetrachords going for him here, and all three of these tetrachords are all-combinatorial tetrachords. That means these tetrachords by themselves can be transposed or inverted (any of the operations that are interval preserving and familiar unto this whole musical syntax) to create a set. This is going to give rise to another aspect of how Schoenberg made choices. (Parenthetically, if you're looking at this piece, you should know that there is a wrong note in the score in m. 35: the B-naturals at the end of the measure should be B-flats. Don't be worried about it. It's a famous, a celebrated, wrong note; the piece by this point becomes so dependent on what's happened earlier in the piece that any kind of a "twelve-count" starting around here is bound to go screwy.) He's ordered the set, the dyads of the set above all, in such a way that when combined with that unique single combinatorial inversion, certain tetrachords result. This gives him a structure of six symmetrically arranged tetrachords that immediately reflects what he did as a purely thematic premise at the beginning of the piece. Notice that the first and sixth, second and fifth, and third and fourth tetrachords are of the same structure. No two of the tetrachords within the same hexachord are of the same structure. The first tetrachord (the "I Got Rhythm" tetrachord) is answered at the end by the sixth tetrachord, and so on.

Here is the point. Schoenberg ordered his hexachords in order to create his usual aggregates. He ordered his discrete dyads in such a way that he would get a symmetry of combinatorial tetrachords which would be reflected in the two-part contrapuntal framework of the piece. The first two measures of the piece, which merely seem to involve an arbitrary thematic presentation of the set followed by its retrograde inversion, reflect the symmetrical repetition structure of that contrapuntal framework. It's a structural idea; it's an idea of continuity; it's an idea of depth; it's an idea of, if you wish, layers of the piece.

There's something else, however, that he's done to get a kind of linear variety in the set itself. This is a piece in which you don't go anywhere nearly as far afield as you do in the Fourth Quartet. It's a tiny piece. Notice one thing, however, that he's done. Consider the tetrachord which consists of E♭, F, A♭, B♭ (the first tetrachord in example 3-11). You can think of it as two major seconds a perfect fourth apart or, of course, as always in such cases of inversional symmetry, two perfect fourths a major second apart. You can always do that with any symmetrical structure. When he split them in the first tetrachord, he chose to state the fourths. In the comparable place in the sixth tetrachord, he chose to state the seconds to get that kind of detailed variety. The chromatic tetrachord can be minor seconds a major second apart or major seconds a minor second apart. In the second tetrachord he states the minor seconds; and in the fifth tetrachord he doesn't state the major seconds, because he can't. There's no way he can do it. All that he can do in the fifth tetrachord is change the order of the minor second. If you want to know why he can't do it, the answer takes us a little deeper, to a fundamental principle. In S_0, he can't state the F where the A♭ is or the F♯ where the G is, because F and F♯ have already been used as part of the set. If you wonder why he can't go back in S_0 to the B and replace it with a D, it's because that will give him the same kind of contradiction, a reflection of the combinatorial structure of the set. He can't, so he gets the variety of the different directions of the minor second. In the third tetrachord, he has minor thirds a major second apart; in the fourth tetrachord, he has major seconds a minor third apart. All of these distinctions are going to affect the degree of difference and the degree of similarity that you get. In other words, at the point when you reach the fourth tetrachord, you're going to start to have similarity of tetrachord type, but difference in modes of linear progression.

The big example of preparing where a piece is going to go in absolutely monumental detail is the opening of *Moses and Aaron. Moses and Aaron*, after all, is a long, long opera. It's two acts long and it's incomplete. Schoenberg spends the first six measures preparing what is going to be the functional interval of the piece in a number of different ways which define the processes of the piece. Now one of the things that has been talked about a great deal about this music is that when a piece begins, you're not really defining the themes of the piece, and you're not defining simply the pitch materials or the intervallic materials; you're also defining the processes of the piece. This again is all part of the notion of contextuality. You're defining how things are going to be made to be related, how transformations are going to take place. All I want to do is show you a little bit of the opening (see example 3-12, on the following page).

Moses and Aaron is utterly unlike the other two pieces we've looked at. Totally different criteria are relevant here, and, up to a certain point, much more of the sort that are characteristic of purely contextual non-twelve-tone music. You might think the opening is a little bit like Opus 33a; it is a little bit, but only very vaguely so. You're not getting very much of the twelve-tone notion out of it, but you get a vaguely similar kind of association. The

I. Akt | Act I

EXAMPLE 3-12

two pairs of opening chords have the same outer voices and the same inner interval.

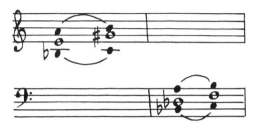

EXAMPLE 3-13

What would you make of something like that? Already Schoenberg expects you to hear a kind of reinforcement of an interval. What that interval is might not be quite obvious yet. When he's given you the opening chords and the ascending quintuplets in measures 3 and 5, he's prepared for you most of the material of a two or two-and-a-half hour piece.

The next stage is something absolutely crucial—something that you haven't seen before and which has been the grounds for criticism, by the way. The criticism is the very simple one that the basis which you need to progress into the piece depends on material, modes, and processes which are presented to you so quickly that you just simply can't handle it. What would you say is the interval that seems to be presented in the foreground of this piece? He's showing you different ways in which the minor third is going to play a role in this piece. The interval between the E–G♯ major third and the D♭–F major third in the opening chords is a minor third. The first and last notes of each quintuplet are related by a minor third—from E♭ to F♯ in the first and from F♯ to D♯ in the second. Their deliberate juxtaposition links them.

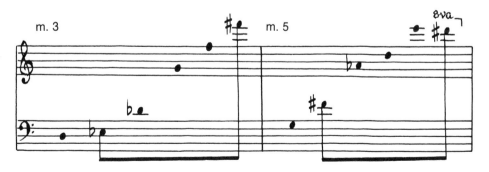

EXAMPLE 3-14

When you finally get a direct statement of what will be dispositionally defined to be the set of the piece, here's what you get: from the first note to the last note is a minor third which is also the interval of the combinatorial inversion (I_3) which plays the kind of role in this piece that it does in all Schoenberg's other pieces.

EXAMPLE 3-15

Now look back at example 3-13. In each pair of chords, the top note of the first chord is A and the bottom note of the second chord is C. This repetition of pitch classes is no coincidence, and it's only the first of such repetitions articulating that interval, the interval that is going to be the basis of relationships between motives of the same content. While it relates top to bottom in those chords, in the quintuplets of example 3-14 it similarly relates first to last: E♭ to F♯, F♯ to E♭. Then in example 3-15, the A to C within each set—again first to last—is not coincidentally the same as the A to C from the first note of one to the first note of the other.

From this point on everything is done associatively. Look at measure 6.

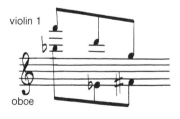

EXAMPLE 3-16

You get three notes as a line in the first violin distinguished registrally and instrumentally: A, D, G. But you can't possibly get A, D, G as a succession from the twelve-tone set. This is a problem for people who try to count to twelve and don't follow the piece through as it evolves associatively. You can't possibly trace the line A–D–G back to any aspect of the set that you've had so far. Similarly, the oboe in the same place has the succession Bb–Eb–Gb. Where does the succession D–G come from? Where do you get a perfect fourth in this set? But you can see where this all comes from if you look at S_0 together with I_3 (see ex. 3-15). D and G are opposite each other, which Schoenberg makes explicit by making them the pickups to the quintuplet. They also occur in comparable places in the quintuplet. Eb and Gb also occur opposite each other in the two set forms. So, in only six measures of the piece, you already have a set of associations by metrical means, rhythmical means, and transpositional means which begin to set up successions in instruments and register that you couldn't possibly have found by going back and counting up to twelve.

What happens when Moses enters is a thing we can't go into in any detail. You get a series of chords—each a tetrachord—so you get six chords constituting two successive set forms.

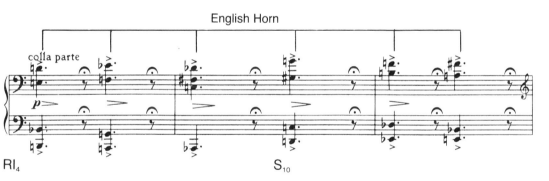

EXAMPLE 3-17

These two forms are not combinatorial. They are the only two set forms from which one can extract one note from each of their tetrachords to yield the middle hexachord of the original set, a hexachord that we've already heard many times—for example, in the bass part in measure 3 (example 3-12). The English horn (highest part in example 3-17) plays one note from each tetrachord of RI_4 and S_{10}; this line taken as a whole replicates the content of that middle hexachord. It is the upper voice in this passage, and it's perfectly clear when you hear it from the pit. It associates two sets which are not combinatorial and which are going to create the Moses collection. Later in the opera, he begins to juxtapose other retrograde-inversionally related sets at that same transposition level. They are not combinatorial, of course, and you can go quite nuts figuring out how he ever got there, unless you look at the beginning of the piece. Aaron's sets are always combinatorial—they are inversionally related sets that begin a minor third apart. Moses' sets are retrograde-inversionally related and are not combinatorial, but they still begin a minor third apart. And so it goes.

4 Questions of Partitioning

I want to get a little more deeply into things that we've covered not only superficially but also in such a way as to give emphasis primarily to local applications. I'd like to start with what happens beneath the surface of combinatorial hexachords. We start with Schoenberg and with hexachords which have certain kinds of inversional combinatorial properties which enable you to create aggregates. That immediately gives you a kind of flexibility beneath the surface, a counterpoint or a harmony in which the components are two segments of individual sets, related to each other inversionally. We've also seen that we can do this with prime and retrograde-inversional combinatoriality (retrograde is obviously trivial).

What I'd like to try to do here is say something about what takes place when you go beyond the immediate applications. If you combine two set segments, you have a certain kind of flexibility with regard to the counterpoint and the harmony, and with regard to ordering. You break down a simplistic linearity, if I may use that expression. The remarkable thing about combinatorial hexachords is that they seem to display their effectiveness over regions totally different and perhaps unrelated from any immediate point of view.

EXAMPLE 4-1

85

In example 4-1 you see a hexachord.[1] It's a hexachord that I happen to have used in a couple of pieces, but that's not the reason that it's here now. It's a first-order hexachord, one which has remarkable characteristics insofar as it is the only such hexachord that cannot be generated by a single interval. It's a hexachord which somehow doesn't seem to have all the obvious characteristics of symmetry, though the symmetry is clearly there. Now what I want to show you is that somehow the relationship between trichords and hexachords generates unexpected constancies or, if you wish, invariants. I want to look at the depth in which a pitch function can behave in a piece. Let's look at what I've done in example 4-2a.

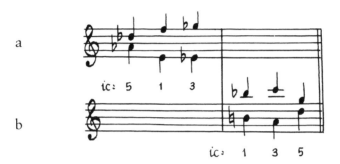

EXAMPLE 4-2

I've taken the second of the trichords of the hexachord in example 4-1 and begun to set up a structural canon by inversion. When I say structural canon, I mean it doesn't have to be a temporal canon like the one in Schoenberg's Opus 16, Number 3. It's a structural canon, in the sense that we've established a contextual relation between the two voices intervallically. How they will occur temporally is yet another structural level or another contextual level beyond that. Then, in example 4-2b, I'm completing the aggregate with yet another canon. Call this a double canon by inversion if you wish. The trichord in example 4-2b is by no possible stretch of the imagination the same as the trichord in example 4-2a; it is, rather, the same trichord type as the last of the trichords of the hexachord in example 4-1. Notice that the hexachord in example 4-2a (and therefore the complementary hexachord in example 4-2b) is the same hexachord type as the one in example 4-1.

I don't want to seem to be displaying some enormous virtuosity. I want you rather to try to intuit—and I do mean that—the kinds of harmonic containments that arise as a result of this interplay between the trichord and the hexachord. At the beginning of this canon, I've simply indicated what I would call qualitative temporality. I mean that the trichords in example 4-2a are going to precede those in example 4-2b, but what happens within these particular delineations is a matter of more highly contextual rhythmic decisions.

The notes in example 4-2a form a hexachord; example 4-2b has the complementary hexachord; together they form an aggregate. Notice that this particular situation of note-against-note, two-part counterpoint results in exactly the same dyad intervals (to within complementation) in example 4-2a as in example 4-2b (ic 1, ic 5, and ic 3) despite the fact that the trichords are totally different. Now we're talking about purely musical resources: pitches and collections. These are resources that you, as a composer, can work with. They wouldn't seem particularly abstract if I had simply said, "We have a canon going here. Now we're going to collect these into the same harmony in some sense." In fact, the repetition of the dyads is simply built into the fact that these two trichords can generate the same hexachord under the operations of the system. And here we begin to get into real compositional issues.

I'm not going to play this, because this is not music. This is no more what I would consider a composition than a second-species counterpoint exercise. You can play such exercises and I could play these note-against-note, but that is not the kind of impression I wish to make. I wish rather to show you how a certain kind of hexachordal containment necessarily creates constancies which are usable, if you wish to use them.

Now notice the next stage. I've purposely laid it out in this way so you can see it as quickly as possible. The continuation of this canon is going to go as in example 4-3.

Those of you who are given to a certain kind of formalism can look ahead and see that you have eight aggregates (numbered 1–8 in example 4-3). Each of the aggregates is determined by having every possible combination of voices, one at a time, two at a time, three at a time, and four at a time. You may regard that as numerical if you wish, but it reflects a spirit of maximum variety, nothing more than that. I don't even know why I wrote it in this

EXAMPLE 4-3

particular registral situation, because register here is taken to be undefined. If these were done in numbers, perhaps I could avoid some of those registral prejudices, but I do think that's less intuitive.

Look again at the hexachord in example 4-1. It consists of four very different trichords. When I say very different, I mean they're not permutations of one another. They're not trichords that could be related by operations on order or by any other of the twelve-tone transformations. Now notice something else regarding what this particular disposition of pitch classes has also retained. The Db–F–Gb in example 4-2a is at the same level as the second trichord in the hexachord in example 4-1. Notice that the other three trichords in examples 4-2a and 4-2b are not at the same level as in the hexachord. The lower trichord in example 4-2b, for example, is T_5I of the last trichord in the hexachord. So already we're getting new levels being defined by certain kinds of containments. Now why should this happen? Is it accidental? Is that something which I've concocted by virtue of a certain kind of ordering? Not at all—it's independent of ordering. The trichords marked in example 4-1 are so different from each other that they don't even have an ordered interval in common. In the first, the intervals are 4 and 1; in the second, they are 2 and 7. And yet the fact does remain that when we continue this inversional half-canonic relationship between them, as in the second aggregate in example 4-3, A is still against C, G is still against D, and Bb is still against B♮, although we've changed the order of the dyads. This is real contextual counterpoint or contextual harmony. This hexachord happens to be the one that I used in both *Partitions* and *Post-Partitions*, and, in a certain sense, this partitioning is exactly what I do with it.

If you look at example 4-4, you'll see that the third trichord is being used in addition to the first trichord.

EXAMPLE 4-4

In other words, example 4-4 involves all of the other trichords. Notice that all the things we've talked about still maintain. As example 4-5 points out, the new canon begins with the third trichord untransposed from example 4-1 (F, Gb, Ab) and continues with the first trichord transposed down a major second, or, if you wish, at t = 10.

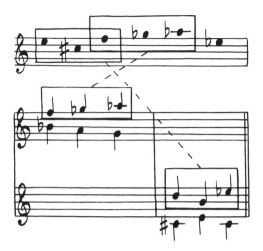

EXAMPLE 4-5

This transposition permits the completion of the aggregate, but it also does more than that. It begins to define how a piece would move within certain kinds of boundary conditions.

Though these relations have been used and probably will be used in many pieces in precisely this form, the rather formalistic canonic way I have set this up suggests that this is still precompositional. I hope you know what I mean when I say precompositional. I don't mean this is something a composer does before he composes his piece. It's not a chronological statement. Precompositional means that it is in a form where it is not yet compositionally performable. You still have to do things to it. You have to assign exact temporal values to these notes. You have to assign registral values. You have to assign timbral values. This is in a theoretical—or, if you wish, in a compositional— state which is not yet performable. Therefore it is *pre*compositional because obviously it's not a formed composition. You have to make further decisions with regard to every element presented here.

Take, for example, the circled G on top of the first system in example 4-3. Now that G is a member of at least four aggregates. In other words, it's a member of at least four structures which mirror each other in a rather—I don't want to say obvious way—a rather decisive way. First, the G is the last element of a lyne indicated by upward stems in the upper stave of the first system. I don't know whether you know this word or not. Michael Kassler derived it from computer work. Lyne in this sense doesn't mean an instrumental line, a registral line, or a dynamically defined line, although it could be projected as any of those things. It is a precompositional lyne, one which you are probably going to project in the piece. Somehow it's going to be projected, but we have a choice of modes of projection. That G is also a part of the aggregate starting with the A–B♭–D in the previous measure. Further, the G is part of an aggregate starting under the circled 3 with the A♭–E– E♭ and continuing, with all the upward-stemmed notes, into the next system. With the trichord of the preceding bar (A–B♭–D), it's also a part of an aggregate formed with the two trichords of the first bar of the next system.

I'm not trying to overwhelm you with numerical facts. Rather, I'm trying to show how you get certain reflections, which, I assume, are going to have to be interpreted compositionally. The main problem, or at least the main property or attribute, is that that G has at least four functions which are very much parallel, very much related. It is part of an aggregate in terms of its own linear extension derived by applying the operations of the system (top staff; upward stems [1–4 and 3–6]), in terms of combination with another voice with the same trichord (top staff; upward and downward stems), and in terms of the combination of these voices with two other voices which are dealing with a different trichord (top staff with bottom staff). That's both the kind of variety and the kind of unification that is available here.

Would anyone be willing to stick his neck out and indicate why these particular transpositional levels were chosen? Look at that original hexachord, and then go back and look at the top and bottom portions of example 4-4, and tell me what they have in common beyond the obvious fact that I've chosen the four trichords from the same hexachord, exhausting it as a trichord source. Think of it like an abstract sketch. I don't mean to imply for a moment that I think of this as being an analog with anything in tonal music— I would hate to say that. This is very much a twelve-tone condition. Can you see what else is being maintained? First, the trichords have to generate the same hexachord to make this possible. No two different trichords generate the same collection of hexachords, but they might generate a hexachord in common, and these all generate a hexachord in common. The levels of these trichords are so chosen that the pitch collection of the original hexachord is maintained. Now if you look at example 4-2a, you will see that this is easily achieved by having that original level of the trichord D♭–F–G♭ answered by A♭–E–E♭. Those six pitch classes constitute the total hexachord of example 4-1. This would not be possible with the trichords in example 4-4 (013 and 014), because the hexachord which they share is not a hexachord of the type which we have in example 4-1. The hexachord they share is a chromatic hexachord. But if you look linearly at example 4-4, you'll notice that by choosing the correct intervallic level, the first two statements in the upper part do indeed outline the original hexachord. So, throughout all of these relationships, either linearly or simultaneously, you can maintain the pitch collection of the original hexachord.

The crux here is the relationship between trichords and hexachords. Why, for example, should there be this maintenance of those dyads? Why should the B♭ against B (in aggregate 1 on bottom staff of example 4-3) recur as B♭ against B (in aggregate 2 on top staff)? The same thing happens in example 4-4. If C♯ occurs against D once, it will do so again. The same is true of the other dyads. There's nothing trivial about that. It happens because of the symmetrical nature of the hexachords, which the trichords share. This property affects everything that's ever done in the chromatic domain. We could have been talking about it with regard to Schoenberg Opus 16 as well as with regard to a twelve-tone piece. It's not intuitively obvious. Take any two trichords. A trichord has three different intervals, but it's impossible to find two trichords which will give you all six intervals. I'm now talking about content intervals, not ordered intervals. There's nothing obvious about that. It means if you have two trichords (and you're constantly dealing with two trichords one way or another—linearly, contrapuntally, or otherwise), there's going to be one interval repeated and that is going to weight your relationship.

Do you all agree with that statement? Can you find two trichords which will together add up to six intervals? Well, let me tell you, you can't. This is one of these mysterious things about the chromatic system. At first, one might think it would work with two trichords which seem to have nothing in common. But no matter what two trichords you take, you're going to have some interval repeated, either within one or between the two. So that means no matter what you do, if you have two trichords, you're going to have a weighted interval. And the weighted interval is obviously going to affect the sound of the piece and the sound of the progression and the sound of whatever you happen to be dealing with.

For example, look as a composer at that G in the top line of example 4-3. As I mentioned, that G functions in at least four dimensions as an element of an aggregate, as an element of a twelve-tone collection, as an element of a chromatic completion. How do you project the different functions of that G? That G (and virtually any other note there) functions in these four different ways. That is one of the things that creates, obviously, a complication in the piece. You can create ambiguity. You can disambiguate it at some other point and make it clear how this G was functioning. You can write a straightforward piece which exploits exactly this. Then you're going to have no problems, but you won't be using a great deal of the richness available to you here.

What I wanted these examples to show is the relationship between combinatorial hexachords and any trichord in the world. I don't care what kind of a set you're dealing with or whether you're dealing with a set at all, but once you begin to generate the complete chromatic from a trichord, you're bound to get all-combinatorial hexachords. They're bound to arise, whether you ever postulated them or not, whether you ever cared about them or not. And they're going to arise quite differently from the way they would if they were just generalizations of Schoenbergian inversional hexachords, which, of course, don't have quite all the properties of all-combinatorial hexachords.

Think of the ways you can generalize from a Schoenbergian inversional hexachord. The first way you can generalize is by going to the all-combinatorial hexachord, which combines and creates aggregates with any possible form of the set. The other way you can go is towards tetrachords and trichords which have the same property. So now let me show you a couple of other things about all-combinatorial sets. I'll show you how different the three first-order all-combinatorial sets are, now that we see they can be resultants rather than just subjects. Look at the hexachord in example 4-6.

EXAMPLE 4-6

It's the all-chromatic hexachord. It was used by Webern in many different ways and also by a lot of the rest of us. You can hear it in my Second Quartet and my *Reflections for Piano and Tape*, although not in that ordering. Can anybody see why this ordering is better than Webern's ordering in the *Symphony* or the *Piano Variations*? It's the only such hexachord in the world which has a certain property. But this property would also hold if we applied the circle of fifths transformation to it to get the diatonic hexachord.

We're dealing with all of this rather artificially, but if you were a composer and you suddenly saw this set and your native language was the twelve-tone language—which is about as reasonable as saying that your native language is Tagalog—you might notice that this hexachord has four different trichords. All four of those trichords, as different as they are, generate that hexachord. There's no other way that you can order that particular kind of hexachord (or, in circle of fifths transform, the diatonic hexachord) that will give you four different trichords all of which generate the hexachord of which they are members. If you look back at example 4-1, you'll discover that the first trichord of that hexachord will not generate the hexachord of which it is a member. It simply will not do it. The others will each generate that hexachord, of which they are all members. Therefore, the only way the first trichord gets into the act—as a generator retaining the pitches of the original hexachord—is by combining it linearly with the fourth trichord, with which it is already combined. Obviously they do share a common hexachord, and the common hexachord which they do share happens to be that chromatic hexachord. I don't like to take this out of a compositional context, so try to think of what this gives you compositionally. Try to think of what this gives you from a standpoint of invariance, of contextual counterpoint. Think of the kind of thing that Schoenberg, within a different set of boundaries, was doing with pieces which were certainly not twelve-tone but which were highly associative.

Do you all see what I meant when I said all four of those trichords in example 4-6, and only those four trichords, would generate the chromatic hexachord? For example, take the first trichord. If you assume that I will not just replicate the example, but will still generate the same hexachordal structure from the trichord, that trichord will take us to a different transpositional level of the hexachord.

EXAMPLE 4-7

I've gotten out of the original, and on I go: I've got a piece going. The second trichord is symmetrical and therefore presents choices. I can go to either of two levels.

EXAMPLE 4-8

I'm following each trichord with its transposed inversion. I could have used the retrograde inversion, but for now we're concerned about content. The ordering will occur at yet a different level of structure. That is not a trivial observation, because you will have different kinds of choices which you can make while still preserving this particular invariance. The third trichord also presents two choices.

EXAMPLE 4-9

I can begin the inversion either on D♯ or C♯. Each would carry me towards a different harmonic area. For the fourth trichord, I don't have that kind of choice because it's nonsymmetrical, but I can still generate the hexachord.

EXAMPLE 4-10

This may look like a lot of mechanics that I've grabbed out of my bag of mechanical tricks. But notice how different choices can carry you to different regions. These may or may not have much in common with the original region; if not, they carry you away from your original region, but by virtue of something contained within it. This can become an extremely powerful instrument of motion in a piece. It means that something which is within the original ordering will carry you to a region which replicates the original region from a standpoint of collection but is a transposition of it. You've got two ways of approaching this situation. You can begin with a trichord either at its original transpositional level and be carried out of the original hexachord or at a new transpositional level and stay within the original hexachord. As an instance of the first approach, we began example 4-7 with the trichord at its original transpositional level: the hexachord in example 4-7 spans from D to G, whereas the original hexachord in example 4-6 went from C to F. If, however, you wanted to remain where you were, we can begin on another transpositional level of the trichord.

EXAMPLE 4-11

The content of the hexachord is equivalent to that of example 4-6. But either way the relation between trichord and hexachord provides criteria for movement. Now let's consider the first-order all-combinatorial hexachord in example 4-12.

EXAMPLE 4-12

That's the one which is quite different from the chromatic and diatonic hexachords because, under a circle-of-fifths transformation, it maps into itself. It maps into its complement by a tritone transposition. It provides a number of paths of hierarchization through which we can move. Now suppose you tried to construct this hexachord in an ordering so that, like the one in example 4-6, each of its trichords can generate the hexachord. Such an attempt would tell you a great deal about the different properties of each of these configurations, configurations which in other ways share properties which are obviously very powerful. You would find, however, that it simply can't be done. In other words, with this hexachord we are dealing with a whole different contextual basis of hierarchization. On the other hand, this hexachord can be ordered so that *none* of its four trichords will generate the original hexachord. This is yet another world because it will take you into a whole different series of different structures. This may seem like a kind of musical game, but once you're involved in a piece, whether you're working explicitly with these materials or not, it gets you into very, very strange lands indeed and makes you wonder why certain things are happening. No matter how much experience you've had with this musical language, you are constantly finding that specific orderings of specific kinds of configurations lead you to certain kinds of constrictions and associations you could never have foreseen. Example 4-13 is a hexachord which has the remarkable property that each of its trichords, by process of derivation, must take you into a totally different structure.

EXAMPLE 4-13

None of them could possibly generate the original hexachord. I'm getting awfully tired of spewing out properties, but this is what's bound to happen when you don't have time to look into the manifestations in individual works (which takes a long time). But at least you do see how, at a certain much more subtle level of relationship, the hexachords in example 4-6 and example 4-13, which have the same combinatorial properties (they are both first-order sets), have very different extension, or developmental, properties. The first trichord of the hexachord in example 4-1 is expressed very explicitly in *Partitions*, and I hesitate to say that this is pure coincidence. Of the trichords, it is the only trichord which will not generate the hexachord of which it is a member. The last section of the piece—both in order to gain homogeneity and to use this particular trichord—is concerned only with that trichord. That is not all that the piece is concerned with, but it certainly is one component with which it is concerned.

Let's go on to something which looks very theoretical and turns out to be very realistic. I would feel conscience-stricken if we didn't deal with this issue, because it has more to do with what happens in real compositions than almost anything else I could come up with. We have talked about various generalizations of the Schoenbergian hexachord. With all-combinatorial hexachords you can create more aggregates in more different ways and therefore more surface orderings in more different ways. But now we're going to generalize in a different way. Why should the set be partitioned only into two parts of six notes each? After all, we're dealing with a kind of contrapuntal situation in which there are lines, and these lines can be partitioned—depending upon the number of parts that you assume (and that would depend upon the piece and what you can project and the instruments and a lot of other things)—into at least twelve parts. Example 4-14 shows you an array of partitions which is the first of a collection of arrays which would show all the partitions of the twelve-tone set into seventy-seven parts.

EXAMPLE 4-14

The number twelve can be partitioned in seventy-seven different ways. The number itself is of no significance—I'm telling you that merely because it happens to be a very simple numerical fact of life. Example 4-14 shows twelve different partitions which would be the first of some six sets of partitions of all seventy-seven. Now if you ever went out and tried to find all seventy-seven partitions of a given set, you might find that this would be rather difficult. No one has yet been able to program a computer to do it, I'm delighted to be able to say. I'm not anticomputer, but every once in a while I like to remember that I can do things a computer can't. Across the top of example 4-14 you will see the usual notation for partitions. Those numbers are not exponents in any usual mathematical sense. Rather, they tell you the number of parts and the number of components in each part. 3^2, for example, means that there are two parts which have three elements each. This is absolutely standard notation, and any of you who have done any combinatory theory will recognize it as such.

I'm showing you this to tell you something absolutely unexpected about that most familiar of operations, inversion. What you have is a series of aggregates. The aggregates are exactly the same as the Schoenbergian aggregates or the Webernian aggregates, except now the number of parts is greater and the variety is greater. No two aggregates have the same number of elements in each linear component. We could have continued this to all seventy-seven, but there's no point in doing it once you understand the purpose involved. One of those aggregates is bound to be 12^1, which would simply be a form of the set. Another one of the aggregates is bound to be 1^{12}, which means there would be one element in each part.

With all the associative properties we've seen in various non-twelve-tone as well as twelve-tone pieces, we know that what we have in this array is a circle of similarities. A dyad like the B–G♭ (upper right-hand corner) can be ordered in any way without violating the underlying norm of the set. A dyad like the F–E (lower right-hand corner) can be ordered in only this one way. And the G–D (beginning of lines 5 and 6) can be ordered as the G–D of line 11, measure 3, or any way you wish. Therefore, we can move from one place on the array to another in a kind of circle of identities. On the other hand, there will be certain aggregates, like the 6^2 (which is the Schoenbergian aggregate structuring), the order of which is highly constrained. And therefore, we'll have to create in some way its similarity through a chain of similarities, through degrees of similarity, through progressive similarities, and a lot of other things. And now we're getting into real music. Away from that "primitive" Schoenbergian stuff.

In example 4-15, I've written out the inversions of the lines from example 4-14. I've inverted each line so as to maintain the combinatorial hexachord.

Aggregates:

EXAMPLE 4-15

The set that I used here is an all-combinatorial, all-interval set using the chromatic hexachord: I tried to take the most weighted set possible, the hottest set, where we could see all of these properties more or less simultaneously. I purposely picked this one because it's also the easiest intuitively to grasp. Further, it happens to be what I use in *Reflections* and, by a strange coincidence, in a much earlier piece, the Second String Quartet. Nobody could have possibly foreseen what happens as a result of what I've done. Across the first line you'll see the inversion $(T_{11}I)$ whose hexachord is identified with the first hexachord in example 4-14. But now, look what happens within those columns which once contained beautiful, marvelous aggregates. My aggregates have disappeared.

Why have I lost my aggregates even while retaining the combinatorial features of the individual lines? If you look on the right, you'll see why: associated with each of those inversions is a different index number—11, 1, 3, 5, 7, 9—in fact, every possible index number. An even index number would be impossible because it would hold a note fixed. Let me show you how nontrivial this mapping is. The relationship between example 4-14 and example 4-15 involves a very complex transformation, a transformation that has properties that we've never encountered before but which are all within what we've quite rudimentarily, or at least primitively or primally, regarded as fundamental operations of the traditional twelve-tone system. As an example, take the B of the sixth aggregate (or sixth column) in example 4-14 and move it back to the preceding aggregate. Then to keep aggregates intact, move the B in line 10 from the fifth to the sixth aggregate. Notice that we haven't changed any specifications of the original counterpoint. Those aggregates are created from twelve-component lines. They had to be constructed. They define a kind of qualitative rhythm. The aggregates are still aggregates, so nothing significant has changed with regard to the boundary conditions. Our changes will make something change musically at another level when we assign these lines to instruments or to registers or to whatever it be. It will be musically different, but not different at this level of specificity.

But look what happens to the comparable notes in example 4-15. The D in line 3 will move from the sixth to the fifth column, and the Ab in the fifth column will move to the sixth. Those weighted aggregates will be changed considerably. Partial aggregate number 6 in example 4-15 will now have an Ab, which it didn't have before, and the fifth aggregate will now have a D, which it didn't have before. So, you see, it's not one-to-one. A choice that you make with regard to how you align aggregates originally will very much affect what you get under the transformation in example 4-15.

This is not what one would call familiar material, although it has been published. It gets us into something which is purely a terminological problem. Why do you want to call the columns in example 4-15 aggregates? They're not aggregates, because they no longer contain all twelve pitch classes, but they're derived from aggregates. However, they've become weighted aggregates in the sense that certain pitch classes are going to appear more than once, and therefore certain pitch classes won't appear at all. This is going to affect the sound of the piece like crazy, of course. And yet what you're doing is transforming the total collection in example 4-14 by a most familiar operation, by simple inversion, an inversional operation which preserves exactly what Schoenberg did when he continued and formed a secondary set. So from this rather traditional assumption you have arrived at something very different. Notice, by the way, certain things that happen here which I just threw in to be amusing. Dyads, for example, are preserved in some of these. C to B (ex. 4-14, line 1, column 1) becomes B to C (ex. 4-15, line 1, column 1), and D to

A (ex. 4-14, line 1, column 2) becomes A to D (ex. 4-15, line 1, column 2). That's not built into the system; that's just an additional plus thrown in there for more fun and games.

Now we go into the real fire. Obviously, if you want to preserve an aggregate, you have to choose an index number which will preserve the aggregate. I will show you how index numbers can have a totally different kind of influence on music from what you may be familiar with. In example 4-16, I applied index number 0 to example 4-14.

I.N. = 0

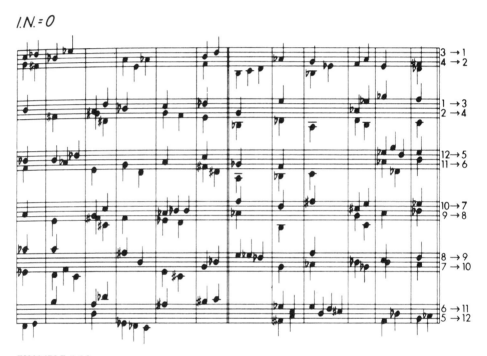

EXAMPLE 4-16

That operation does preserve the vertical aggregates, as you can see. Look at the first elements of the top line of examples 4-14 and 4-16: index number 0 maps 0 into 0 (0+0=0), 11 into 1 (11+1=0); now look at the second lines: 5 into 7 (5+7=0), 6 into 6 (6+6=0), and so on. I did the same thing to each successive aggregate. When I did so, I retained my lovely lines, which are forms of what I had as lines in my first collection but shifted in their relative position in the total array. I've shown how that is done by the mapping numbers on the right side of example 4-16. We have a series of mappings of lines onto lines. For example, what was the third line in example 4-14 (a hexachord ranging from B♭ to E♭) now becomes the first line in example 4-16. This is indicated by the mapping number 3 to 1. Notice also that the mapping by inversion preserves ordering. If it didn't, we wouldn't be talking about the same thing at all. Earlier, we inverted the lines, which after all is a very familiar form of inversion. Here, we're inverting the collection, the aggregate. The difference, of course, is that we preserve the aggregates, but we shift the position of the lines according to a pattern which is exactly like the pattern that happens to notes when you invert a set. What first applied to pitch classes now applies to total sets. We now see a progression from the single pitch class to the total set, and we begin our ascent into musical structure. Certain things happen which are exactly like the effect of inversion on individual pitch classes. If 3 maps into 1, then 1 maps into 3. If 4 maps into 2, then 2 maps into 4. If 12 maps into 5, 5 maps into 12. 'Tain't trivial. These are complete lines, but they map in pairs, just as pitches do. We have now made the giant leap.

Look at example 4-17, where I chose an odd index number and did the same thing. Notice that, in this case, 1 maps into 1, and 2 maps into 2, but the others get scrambled.

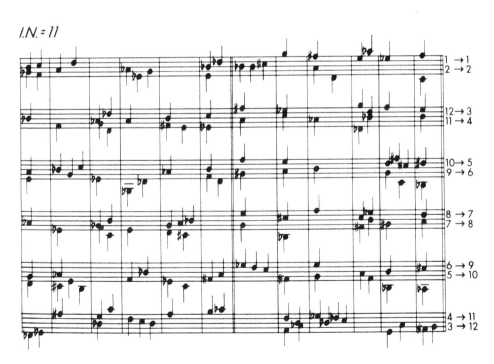

EXAMPLE 4-17

The mapping is: 1 maps into 1, 2 maps into 2, 8 maps into 7, 7 into 8, and so on. 12 maps into 3, and 3 maps into 12, and, a tritone away, 6 maps into 9, and 9 maps into 6. Similarly, the mapping of 5 and 10 is a tritone away from the mapping of 4 and 11. This is a very mysterious property, by the way, and to demonstrate it is like demonstrating the hexachordal property—it's very difficult to prove. You're not getting incomplete aggregates in examples 4-16 and 4-17, but you're rearranging the lines. The compositional applications of this are quite literally infinite. Suppose, for example, you're writing a piece in which one instrument is primary and can trace through. If it traces through under these maintenances of aggregates with all of its original linear associations, it can pass through every possible partitional part. But since these examples present only one of six arrays needed to get the seventy-seven possible partitions, you'd be chasing through some rather lengthy partitions. This is just the beginning of the real compositional applications of these ideas.

QUESTION: When you say these properties are mysterious, that has a lot to do with the way I feel about properties I come up with in some of the same ways perhaps. Do you find any intuitive way of thinking about, say, the way those sets mapped onto each other? Does *mysterious* mean that you can't find anything intuitive?

No, on the contrary. Intuitively, it seems to me perfectly clear why this is an extension of the notion of inversion from individual elements to sets. But if you tried to demonstrate this, or to prove this in abstract terms, as with the hexachordal theorem, you would find the proof is very difficult.

You all know the hexachordal theorem so I'm not going to belabor you with it, but let me give you some of the background. David Lewin came to Princeton having been an undergraduate major in mathematics at a certain vocational school on the Charles River. I don't know anybody in the world brighter than David Lewin. David Lewin came to Princeton to study class field theory with the famous mathematician Emil Artin. He spent about a week as a graduate student in the mathematics department—a very special kind of hothouse, let me tell you—and then came over to the music department. He felt he didn't want to spend his life doing just mathematics, because he had lots of other things he could do. But he brought with him a kind of mathematical equipment which I certainly never possessed.

At one point, we began thinking about how you would prove the hexachordal theorem, which maintains that complementary hexachords have the same multiplicity of intervals. So we sat and we worked for many a week together. We were typically equipped amateurs in mathematics (though David, God knows, had technique that I didn't have), and we found a solution. We used topological methods. We hit this little problem with all kinds of heavy hammers, and we solved it. Anyway, one day, I was speaking to a man named Ralph Fox, who was one of the great knot theorists of the world. (Knot theory is a very complicated field of topology.) At a summer mathematics workship here in Madison, he'd heard about the property from a colleague of his who'd been told about it by George Perle, then at the University of Louisville. He said, "This is a very interesting problem. Have you solved it?" I showed him our proof and he said, "My God, I don't even understand your proof." What he was saying was that amateurs use such heavy-handed methods. He also realized very quickly, as we had by then, that the hexachordal theorem was a generalization of the complementation theorem, which asserts that the weighting of the intervals will be the same for any complementary sets, regardless of the partitioning. No matter how you partition, no matter how many notes you take out, you're going to have that intervallic weighting remaining the same between and among the parts.

About two weeks later, Ralph called me up and he said, "Milton, I think I've got a general solution for this. And not only is it a terrific solution but it's going to help me crack Waring's problem." Waring's problem is one of the old standing problems in number theory. And by finding a very elegant proof, using group theory, to solve our little empirical musical problem very simply, he had solved Waring's problem. Strangely enough, David and I certainly knew enough group theory to do it ourselves, but we didn't know how to use it. Well, Ralph invited us to hear him present the proof to the math club. He began his presentation by saying that these musicians had suggested a problem in partitions and interval weighting, and that's why we were there. This issue is very esoteric for mathematicians because it would never occur to them to subtract numbers. That's why the all-interval set makes no sense to them at all, of course. We subtract numbers and call the results intervals, but there is no particular reason why this should ever arise in mathematics. Anyway, he showed the proof and it was wonderful: it was very elegant. It was published as a new way of solving Waring's problem. In order to solve our problem, he had solved one of the really classical mathematical problems.

At one point in the presentation, Ralph tried to tell the mathematicians what musicians call an interval. He said, "You count up from one note to another and you've got an interval. Here's one they used to call a major third, but they now call it a four." Then he turned to me and he said, "Milton, this is really funny. You call these major thirds or fours, but there's no name whatsoever when they're at a zero." I said, "Yes, we call it a unison." He said, "I never heard that before!" Such were our different worlds.

Ralph Fox died soon thereafter. David Lewin then published his own proof, with which I had nothing whatsoever to do, using characteristic functions.[2] The essential point is this: once you've seen them, these things seem, intuitively, to be pretty obvious. The problem is to demonstrate that they're universals, or that they're restricted. For example, we have certain invariants which are true of any set anywhere, under all conditions, others which are true of a class of sets such as combinatorial hexachords, and others which are true only in very special cases. For example, I wrote a piece using the only hexachord in the world which has all of its own generators. You can't construct a hexachord with this property except by duplicating my hexachord. In other words, the degree of extension of various of these properties goes from the general to the very specific.

But here's a property that's intuitively very strange. The all-trichordal set is of great value to many composers because it contains ten different trichords, each one of which can generate a set and thus get you from one area into another. There are ten because we drop out the diminished triad, which can't generate a set, and the augmented triad, which is ambiguous under the operations of the system. We could get them, too, by going around the corner, linking end to beginning, but who needs them? It's not hard to write an all-trichordal twelve-tone set. Here is the one from *Images,* my saxophone piece. It has all kinds of excellent properties.

EXAMPLE 4-18

This one, by the way, does not have a 3 or a 9, which might already surprise you. It also happens to be all-combinatorial. Here's another one if you want to compare notes.

EXAMPLE 4-19

This is the one that I used for my Indiana piece, *Ars Combinatoria*, because I was extremely generous with them—I gave them one that has everything.

Now here's what defies intuition totally: it is absolutely impossible to construct an all-trichordal set which is also all-interval. Why should that be? You've got all this intervallic variety—ten different trichords. It seems to me that the two properties should very well conjoin, but they can't. This is where order begins to impose itself upon collection. The ordering necessary to get an all-trichordal set defeats the possibility of an all-interval set. (By the way if there's anybody in this room who can prove this by any so-called mathematical methods, he can beat anybody I know in the field of combinatorial mathematics.) Intuitively, it just doesn't seem right. It shows how deeply these properties of order and collection begin to contradict each other.

Let's talk now about Stravinsky and his verticals. I want to talk about this because it is a genuinely different approach to the twelve-tone issue. Stravinsky established new bases of continuity in hierarchization that could never have dropped out of any kind of twelve-tone issue that we've been discussing. By the way, there are many composers in England and in this country who pursue this whole notion of verticals far beyond anything that you find in Stravinsky. For me, the strategic point to begin with is the fact that you could regard the 12 × 12 array of Schoenberg's as being one which simply could be re-interpreted by one quick shift of the axis as Stravinsky's verticals. That's just a way of viewing it that gives you a sense of the dual interpretation of intervals and pitch classes; it's not, of course, the way Stravinsky conceived of it. He conceived of it as canonic. Stravinsky's first twelve-tone pieces were (I don't want to appear to use this word in any evaluative sense) rather literal. They were what many people commonly think of as twelve-tone pieces. They were twelve-tone motivically, linearly, literally, and in many other ways. Stravinsky's work with all this began with the *Movements*. He obviously realized that he was going to deal with intervals as no one had ever dealt with them before. Now my personal relation to all of this is in my paper; it's public.[3] But I must confess to you that we were never quite prepared for what he did. I'm constantly bowled over (in much the same way that I am by Irving Berlin) by the way in which he did things which he obviously could not have arrived at by any kind of technique (in the sense that we would use the word) with regard to precompositional things.

The immediately exposed set of Stravinsky's *Movements* is this.

H_1 H_2

0   1   7   5   6   11 | 9   8   10   3   4   2   (0 = E♭)

EXAMPLE 4-20

Now already, it's quite remarkable that this is a second-order set. I don't know how he came up with this, but a second-order set has all kinds of special properties. He "intuited" a way of handling the hexachord as a canon in which he transposed each successive note to the initial starting point. In the case of the *Movements*, the starting point is E♭. If you know the *Movements* at all, this is just laid out right at the beginning of the piece.

0	1	7	5	6	11
0	6	4	5	10	11
0	10	11	4	5	6
0	1	6	7	8	2
0	5	6	7	1	11
0	1	2	8	6	7

EXAMPLE 4-21

There are some ideas here which never could have turned up with regard to any other approach that we've talked about. And I do remind you, this is Stravinsky, not some American college professor playing around with esoteric ideas of very strange phenomena. Stravinsky came up with this working canonically within the individual hexachords. It's really remarkable that Stravinsky seized upon hexachords just as Schoenberg, Berg, and Webern had. But he certainly did it in his own inimitable way, after, however, he had already written a number of pieces in which he had dealt with twelve-tone materials in a much more, if you wish, traditional way.

Now the remarkable part of all of this is that the zeros in the first column in example 4-21 are just the zeros of the diagonals in any 12 × 12. The columns of example 4-21 are the diagonals of example 4-22.

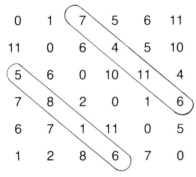

EXAMPLE 4-22

The numbers in the second column of example 4-21 therefore represent the intervals between elements of the set that are one order position apart, the numbers in the third column represent elements two apart, and so on.

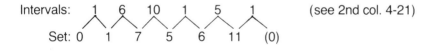

Intervals: 1   6   10   1   5   1   (see 2nd col. 4-21)
Set: 0   1   7   5   6   11   (0)

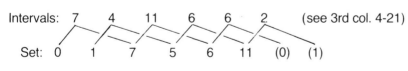

Intervals: 7   4   11   6   6   2   (see 3rd col. 4-21)
Set: 0   1   7   5   6   11   (0)   (1)

EXAMPLE 4-23

This is tremendously intervallically dependent, much more so than anything we saw in Schoenberg or anybody else. Now if the numbers in example 4-20 are intervals, those in the columns of example 4-21 are already intervals between intervals. But they're also pitch classes, and that's one of the things we perhaps didn't emphasize enough when we looked at our 12 × 12. Those numbers are duals: they are both pitch-class numbers and interval numbers, and there's basically no functional difference between the two. The number 6 in the second column, for example, is the interval between 1 and 7 in the original hexachords. At the same time, of course, it is nothing more than a pitch-class number in a particular transposition. All we have in the rows of example 4-21 are six transpositions which have been "rotated." I don't like that expression, because it seems to imply a new kind of operation, and it's not a new operation at all. It's a canon.

Stravinsky seemed to believe from the beginning that he had to construct a particular hexachord in order to get a property which is true of any hexachord anywhere. (This gets us back to the issue of the range of invariance.) The content of the second vertical, as he called it, and that of the sixth vertical are inversionally related, as are the third and fifth. The fourth is inversionally symmetrical with regard to itself. He might have thought he was building in symmetries and associations, but this symmetry is built into the whole twelve-tone condition, because all that he's basically done is transposed and retro-graded. He's transposed order number as well as pitch-class number. Therefore what he has is a succession of complements. After all, the pitch classes diagonally symmetrical with respect to the zero diagonal on a conventional 12 × 12 are by definition complements. In example 4-22, 11 in column 1 is complemented by 1 in row 1, 5 by 7, etc. Therefore, what he has here are symmetries around an origin. And look how obvious the symmetries are in example 4-21. For every 1 in column 2, you have an 11 in column 6. For the 6, 10, and 5 in column 2, you have, respectively, a 6, 2, and 7 in column 6. These pairs all add up to index number 0, so column 2 and column 6 must be inversions of one another with regard to that original 0. So what he has is a series of symmetries of chords around a symmetrical center. Columns 3 and 5 present a similar inversional symmetry with index number 0. The fourth column is symmetrical with regard to itself.

It's a rather extraordinary thing that he came up with. He didn't really believe it was a general property. He thought this was a result of this remarkably constructed hexachord, but it is true of any hexachord, anywhere, anyplace, anytime, no matter what its structure. It's basically a tautology; it's trivially the case. What you're doing, of course, is bringing the next number forward each time: subtracting a larger number in each row from each order position. But that means in each case you're creating a new sort of retrograde: it's a sort of permuted complementation. But what is a retrograde but an order inversion? We know that. So therefore you're creating a succession of inversions where specific order positions identify inversionally related elements: 7 and 4 and 11 and then 6, complemented by 5 and 8 and 1 and then 6, as in example 4-22.

Stravinsky seemed to have had some remarkable insights about this. He seemed to realize that in this collection of verticals there was no 3 and no 9. There's a good reason for that, because he has a second-order hexachord, which contains no 3s or 9s. Those are the boundary intervals. So he started his second hexachord with pitch-class number 9.

H_2

9	8	10	3	4	2
9	11	4	5	3	10
9	2	3	1	8	7
9	10	8	3	2	4
9	7	2	1	3	8
9	4	3	5	10	11

EXAMPLE 4-24

And when you do that, automatically you put a series of 9s in the first column. Remember, he's treating this by analogy with the first hexachord. We're doing exactly the same thing in H_2 with regard to 9 as we do in H_1 with regard to 0. Therefore, there will be a 3 in each of the lines in example 4-24, just as there was a 6 in each of the lines in example 4-21. Notice in example 4-25 that, while the original series, or set, runs across the top line, the lines below it are not necessarily twelve-tone sets.

	H₁						H₂				
0	1	7	5	6	11	9	8	10	3	4	2
0	6	4	5	10	11	9	11	4	5	3	10
0	10	11	4	5	6	9	2	3	1	8	7
0	1	6	7	8	2	9	10	8	3	2	4
0	5	6	7	1	11	9	7	2	1	3	8
0	1	2	8	6	7	9	4	3	5	10	11

EXAMPLE 4-25

The second line, for example, contains two 11s and two 10s. Some will be twelve-tone sets and some will not, depending on the order of the original hexachord. The first, third, and sixth lines are, but the others are not. This gives him a whole new basis of progression, either through the real set or through this new realignment which is founded upon the way he has ordered his second hexachord. It's an extraordinary proposition. Notice that the second 6 × 6 array has a different center of symmetry from the first one. We have a 9 now, not a 0. As with the first array, the second column is symmetric with regard to the sixth, the third with regard to the fifth, and the fourth with regard to itself, but the symmetry is with regard to 9, not 0. Because Stravinsky began the second hexachord with 9, every pitch class occurs the same number of times in the complete array in example 4-25. If he had started with 8 (which wouldn't violate any twelve-tone principle you could think of) that would no longer be true. You'd have six 8s in the second part of the array and two more already in the first part, so you'd no longer have that balance. It's really quite remarkable. To be honest with you, I don't know quite how he came up with this, except just by some kind of inspection.

Notice also that since the hexachord is a second-order set, you're going to have certain permutations of the original. The fifth line in the first 6 × 6 array (0–5–6–7–1–11) is a permutation of the original hexachord. That needn't necessarily happen, but it happens here because of the redundancy of the second-order set. The fifth line of the second array, however, is not a permutation of the second hexachord, because the ordering of the second hexachord is different from the ordering of the first hexachord.

Now look at the verticals for just a moment and consider them as pitch-class numbers. If you interpret them as pitch-class numbers, you immediately get intervals that were never available in the original set. The third vertical, for example, begins 7, 4. If Eb equals 0, which is the realistic thing in this particular piece, 7, 4 will give you Bb, G. Bb to G is an interval of 9, which doesn't occur in the set at all. We've thus got a whole new collection of intervals. The British author Eric Walter White, who wrote a book on Stravinsky, is mystified by a passage where the flute goes Bb–G. He says the interval is "foreign to the series."[4] Well of course it's not in the series. Once you see a 3 or a 9, you know you're dealing with verticals. The 3 and the 9 are the clues that Stravinsky gives you when he's dealing with these materials.

Let's look next at the array of the inversion.

H₁

0	11	5	7	6	1
0	6	8	7	2	1
0	2	1	8	7	6
0	11	6	5	4	10
0	7	6	5	11	1
0	11	10	4	6	5

EXAMPLE 4-26

You get a series of transpositions of the inversion—with the rotational feature—which is exactly what you'd expect. But you also get a lot of other things, too, because by the nature of the ordering of this second hexachord, you're going to get certain identities between the verticals which create yet another basis of relationship. The second vertical in example 4-26 has the same content as the sixth vertical in example 4-25. Similarly, the third vertical in example 4-26 and the fifth vertical in example 4-25 have the same content. You're getting a retrograde of the verticals in content by virtue of direct inversion of the array. We see again the relationship between the retrograde and the inversion, and, more generally, the complex interrelationship between identities and alterations. The inversional array gives you new verticals, but they're not really new. They're just the verticals of the original collection reversed in order as totalities, as collections, and rotated in order in space—vertically—by virtue of the ordering of the inversion. Once you take a progression through these verticals seriously, you're inducing a retrogression of verticals by virtue of inverting the original set.

The *Movements* was the first piece in which Stravinsky made use of these verticals. The only other instrumental piece in which he used them was the *Variations*. Though the rest of the piece is pretty straightforward, the beginning of the *Huxley Variations* is rather mysterious—the first half-dozen measures seem a total scramble. By that, I simply mean if you listen to it, you don't see any kind of associative things happening such as you do here in the *Movements*. Then, at the end of the piece, he states the verticals absolutely explicitly as a series of chords—a striking instance of disambiguation. Kohl, in his article in *Perspectives*, points out that what Stravinsky did in the beginning of the piece was to rotate his complete set.[5] Once you begin applying this vertical technique to the complete set rather than to the disjunct hexachords, you get some pretty remarkable things. There's a case where Stravinsky even uses grace notes to get various kinds of associations.

Let's return to the set for the *Movements*: Eb–E–Bb–Ab–A–D–C–B–C♯–F♯–G–F. It's a second-order set with all the internal relations of such hexachords. Let me show you another second-order set to demonstrate some other possibilities.

EXAMPLE 4-27

The trichords in the second hexachord are different not only from those in the first hexachord but also from each other. It's amazing the way in which these constraints interrelate. If you have a third-order set, there's no way in the world that you can get two different trichords within a hexachord. Given one trichord, the other one has to be the same. You get less and less trichord variety as you get more and more combinatorial potential.

Now consider this set together with its combinatorially related inversion. I could have chosen the inversion beginning either on G or C♯. Now notice

ordered
PC intervals:

EXAMPLE 4-28

the ordered pitch-class intervals created. This is a case where registral choice can give us a real double counterpoint of a very special type that you get only with this kind of a set. There are no intervals in common between the first and second parts of example 4-28, something that will happen only if you have such a set. But the intervals in the second part, when actual registers were chosen, could be a permutation of the intervals from the first part—a very special kind of twelve-tone double counterpoint.

What would happen if you began with four voices, including the retrogrades of the two in example 4-28?

EXAMPLE 4-29

Let's look simply at just the first chord. It can obviously be looked upon as something which is a transposition of a tetrachord within P_0 and therefore could suggest or predict a certain transposition to which we are going. If you choose a second-order, all-combinatorial set, you're going to have a situation of closed intervals, depending upon registral choice and ordering, which will be unlike the intervallic situation with any other all-combinatorial set.

Let me explain what I mean by that. A second-order set can be regarded as consisting of three tritones. When you run such a hexachord against its complement (as I have done in each half of example 4-28), there are going to be just three pairs of intervals in each constructed aggregate. In the first half of example 4-28 we have two 1s, two 3s, and two 5s. The other three odd intervals will always have to occur on the other side, and as you can see, the second half of example 4-28 contains two 7s, two 9s, and two 11s. In each aggregate defined by the two inversionally related hexachords, you're going to produce three intervals, each occurring twice (or, to put it another way, two occurrences each of three intervals). The intervallic content of the two constructed aggregates is discrete; each aggregate is closed with regard to interval content. In other words, by the very nature of the structure of the hexachord, the intervals which occur in the first aggregate (first half of example 4-28) cannot occur in the second aggregate (second half of example 4-28). The hexachord has to contain three tritones for this to be true, and this is the only hexachord which does (except for the whole-tone hexachord, which I never take very seriously).

I said that the intervals in the first half of example 4-28 would have to be distinct from those in the second half, but once you make registral choices in your composition, you could, in literal terms, get the succession 5–1–5–3–1–3 in the second half. In other words, you can get, by registral choice, the registrally defined intervals of one hexachord expressing the structurally defined intervals of the other hexachord—a real double counterpoint. But that depends on registral choice and ordering, and takes us beyond the structural and into the contextual.

Example 4-29 shows the way my *All Set* begins. The ordering here was dependent upon many characteristics of the piece, including the fact that it consists of two saxophones, two brass instruments, two pitched percussion instruments (piano and vibes), the unpitched drums, and the double bass (which functions entirely as a resonator). The whole set was constructed with particular associations in mind. You have two possible choices of transposition to create aggregates. In the first hexachord of the set, each of the two trichords can by itself generate the hexachord of which it's a member—they are of the same trichord type (015). In the second hexachord, the two different trichords together make up a form of the hexachord of which they are members, but neither of them will generate that hexachord. What we have here is a case of a higher-order set in which it is possible to construct a hexachord in which you do not have generators. If you get to the third-order set, no matter how you order it, every trichord will be a generator of the hexachord. There are all these hierarchies whereby the more combinatoriality you get, the more restrictions you get from a certain point of view. In *All Set,* the set juxtaposes two hexachords, which are made distinct in this aspect purely by virtue of ordering.

The piece opens with all of the instruments present and doing exactly what is shown in example 4-29. The fact that the first two pitch classes of P_0 and the first two pitch classes of I_7 together form a major-minor triad (kind of a blues triad) is, of course, idiomatic. Also, this is another indication of how you can adumbrate, or suggest, elements of a different kind of hexachord. For example, in the lower two lines of example 4-29 I could have used the combinatorially related forms a tritone away, so that they would begin D–E♭ and F–E, respectively. If I had done that, I wouldn't have gotten my set segment out of the first elements of each line. In other words, what you want to achieve by way of total harmony or total replication of a segment of the set will already determine the transpositional issues. Having the choice of two combinatorial transposition levels leads to different ways in which these instruments can be paired: either to associate with one another or to complement one another. In this way, the pitch associations are very much determined by the timbral associations.

QUESTION: What are your general feelings about the extent to which the mechanics of the piece need potentially to be able to be inferred from the surface of the piece, and if so, by whom?

As far as I'm concerned, all the things that we have been talking about should be inferrable from the surface. I couldn't possibly stop and say just how at each stage, nor would I feel obliged to. We're talking about degrees of association through pitch and interval, which are, if you wish, the stimuli. The responses to this would involve nothing more than a capacity to perceive, to remember, to apprehend relationships which are relatively traditional. We assume people can understand pitch and intervallic relationships in any music whatsoever. If not, then Mozart and Brahms would be just as unintelligible as would be the examples we have discussed. However, it is perfectly true that the way in which one compounds the sorts of relation we have been discussing in one's memory is very different. Throughout all of this, what I was trying to emphasize, in the most abstract way (because they're all susceptible to a variety, an infinity, of interpretations on the surface), were degrees of affinity and differentiation, the differentiations proceeding by affinity. The Schoenberg Fourth Quartet was an example of these processes. At a certain point, you'd realized that you'd arrived at a stage of the piece which, by pitch association, had been strongly implied by other points in the piece. But when you reached that point, it too had its implications through a different mode of association to another point in the piece. We're talking about the facts, but obviously these facts have their correlating effects. If they didn't have their correlating effects, then there would be no reason to talk about them as facts in the first place.

I could show you a multitude of properties about twelve-tone sets that I am not sure could ever be interpreted musically in such a way as to be (I'm going to be very careful about the word I use) eventually apprehended or usefully apprehended. For Schoenberg, there didn't seem to be any general way of hierarchizing permutations of the total twelve-tone set, and therefore he turned to identifying these sets through retained collections. However, I know of many ways of hierarchizing orders, but I don't see quite how they could be projected musically. Here is an example. It is very well known that complementary transpositions will always retain the same number of order inversions of the original set of which they are transpositions. Now order inversions have nothing to do with inversions in the usual musical sense. If B precedes F♯ in one set form and F♯ precedes B in another, that's an order inversion. You certainly can hear changes of order. Nobody in his right mind would say you couldn't hear them. But the number of them remains fixed if and only if the two transpositions are complementary. Now it's perfectly obvious that you could set out a piece in which you'd stick these things in individual instruments or individual registers, and presumably what you'd hear would be the same number of order inversions. But I can't imagine adding up the number of order inversions; I can't imagine a particular number of inversions as a useful musical property. I have no doubt that somehow you could make some sort of special perceptual property of it; but, in any case, that's the kind of property I mean. There are thousands of those, and I just don't see that they're useful.

There is one piece we didn't have a chance to talk about and maybe this is the place: Schoenberg's Woodwind Quintet. It's an interpretation of a kind of sonata form in twelve-tone terms, in which he definitely uses the notion of degree of similarity as one would in the circle-of-fifths sense. The set is this:

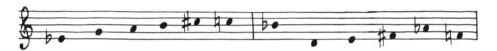

EXAMPLE 4-30

It's one of his combinatorial sets, but it's an extremely redundant set. The second hexachord is virtually a transposition of the first except in the last notes. This is the first real twelve-tone piece he ever wrote, and it's all set out rather simply. Now what he uses for the second theme is not a transposition a fifth above as some have said, but the following:

EXAMPLE 4-31

He uses an inversion which maintains a maximal number of relationships to the original and also a minimal number of changes of order. These relations are the basis of the set form out of which he shapes his so-called second theme—a notion of similarity between two set forms which he thinks is a minimal similarity for this particular set.

On his sketch for the slow movement of the Quintet, Schoenberg wrote "Goethe would have been proud of me." He's a German after all, and here's what Goethe would have been proud of.

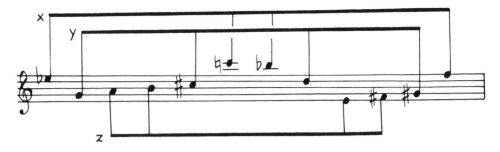

EXAMPLE 4-32

The first time through the set the horn states the line I have marked X while the bassoon states the remaining notes. The second time through, the horn states the line Y while the bassoon states the remaining notes, and then the third time through, the horn states line Z while the bassoon states the remaining notes. He's made a discovery. He says Goethe would have been proud of him, which means he thinks it's pretty clever. Do you see what he's got? He's got three all-combinatorial symmetrical tetrachords by a symmetrical partitioning of his original set. And if you go listen to the Woodwind Quintet, you'll hear them. You can decide for youself whether Goethe would have been proud of him.

5 Professional Theorists and Their Influence

We have produced now at least two generations of professional theorists. I really think of our professional theorists beginning with the generation of Allen Forte. The notion of professional theory is almost totally new. There were virtually no professional theorists in this country, unless you count the people who took degrees at teachers' colleges by counting the number of six-four chords in the *Teutonic* Sonata of Edward McDowell (there were such theses by the way) or those people who found new labels for old chords or old labels for new chords. That's really all that one could call theory. There was no such thing as a professional theorist at any university that I can think of when I began becoming involved with universities.

The idea of taking theory seriously was the result of a couple of things. First of all, it was a result of Schenker and of people who came over here who were Schenker students. It was also the result of much greater interrelationship among the fields, because of the fact they were all in the university. It has to do with the particular milieu which is our country and our particular culture. The idea of serious theoretical thinking about music, analytical thinking worthy of the name of theory (as theory would be worthy of its name in almost every other field except our benighted one), is something new and for which I am grateful. There are probably six magazines now devoted almost entirely to serious theoretical-analytical issues; there were none whatsoever when I began in this racket. There was nobody who was willing to call himself a theorist. There were textbook writers but they weren't theorists. So this is all a very new phenomenon.

I began teaching a History of Theory course in the early fifties in an attempt to make people aware of the fact that there had been theorists who had been very influential in the past, even more influential than any theorist is today (something, by the way, which I do not greet with a great deal of joy). The whole question of theoretical methodology, analytical methodology, and verbal methodology is very close to my heart as a composer, not as a theorist. When I delivered my keynote (or prime set) address to the Society for Music Theory in 1981, the point I really tried to make was that I was very grateful for this new aspect of our lives as composers because it would allow me to stop passing as a part-time theorist and go back to my full-time vocation as a part-time composer.[1] I say that because it simply happens to be literally true, and therefore I repeat it because it's not a joke to be told once. It's a truth to be savored over and over again, though it comes a little late. And, though I'm terribly interested in this, it's wonderful to think that one can no longer read all the articles. There are people around who actually read *Music Theory Spectrum*, who read *Music Forum*! This is a whole new development.

When I taught my History of Theory course, it began as a year course with musicologists and composers; it was later reduced to a single semester. If you really deal with Rameau, you have to deal with Rameau for about four three-hour sessions. He never said the same thing twice in the same way—he constantly changed his mind. It's wonderful: he has a new explanation for the major triad in every book that he ever wrote, and a new explanation for the minor triad; he makes new discoveries. Rameau is a marvelous example of an autodidact. You know what the trouble with autodidacts is—they have such lousy teachers! And poor Rameau was one of these people who have just discovered intellectual life. He was influenced by Leibnitz (a fine guy to be influenced by as far as I'm concerned) and by John Locke. He discovered the overtone series and he was influenced by that.

This kind of nonintellectual history is fascinating, but I could never get very excited about what this had to do with any composer writing. I don't want you to misconstrue my attitude towards this. I'm given to making jokes, but my gratitude to what has gone on in music theory is profound. I was asked to write in a magazine called *High Fidelity* (why do I ever do it?) about the future of music.[2] They asked, on their anniversary, that various people suggest what was going to happen to music in the next thousand years. I was the only composer asked because I'm supposed to know about the future. (I have a Ouija board!) No, they asked me because they thought I was going to talk about technology. I refused to talk about technology. I said whatever the new technology was, it wasn't going to be in the hands of the people anyhow; if we wouldn't have access to it, why talk about it? But I talked about the fact that what I most regretted was that the people who had demonstrated that they were concerned to look at a piece of music and say intelligible things about it, from which (if one wished to) one could at least devolve reasonable and defensible evaluatives, were never consulted. Instead you would still have the ubiquitous journalism and still have the irresponsibles (often performers) determining what could be performed. Asking a performer what should be performed is like asking a printer what book should be published. This is a serious question, and I think that the trouble with music theorists at the moment is they haven't asserted their authority, which is also true in so many other fields. I mean that very seriously.

I can tell you an anecdote about Simon Sechter which is of much greater relevance to our intellectual life than anything I can say. Sechter was a theorist who moved to Vienna (you never forget the date) in 1828 and announced that he was going to teach theoretical courses. You know the first person who signed up for those courses? Schubert. Schubert felt there was a hot new theorist in town, a guy who had new ideas about how music goes, and he went and found out about it. Now, whether he ever got there or not, we don't know. He arranged for a lesson and wrote some exercises for it, but he may have been too ill to attend or he may have had one lesson in November of that year. There's no way to check. He had already written all the works that many people love.

The reason I tell you this story is because of two things: the first one will be anecdotal; the second one will be more relevant. There was a man who was rather more martyred than he deserves, a famous physicist (an infamous physicist for my money), who used to be director of the Institute for Advanced Studies, which happens to reside in Princeton. One day I had a fight with him about why there were no composers or musicians in the Institute. The Institute provides a refuge for all those people who don't need refuge, the physicists, the historians of art, and the economists, who would be very happily treated just as well in universities, as some of us are not. I asked him why there were no composers. He said, "We take people into the Institute who have had to spend years developing their particular capacities. Composers don't have to do that." I said, "What do you mean? There has never been a composer that you have ever heard of who didn't spend years developing his craft, learning either formally or informally, and usually a combination of both." So he came up with the one instance that these people always come up with. He said, "Well, what about Schubert?" And so I said, "Schubert got four years of instruction in counterpoint in the Gymnasium with Salieri" (he'd never heard of Salieri; that was before the play made people aware of him). I said, "We can't even give four years of counterpoint at Princeton, and Salieri was not exactly a stumblebum. Schubert did all of this." And then I told him that when Sechter (whom he'd never heard of either, of course) came to Vienna, the first person to rush and sign up to study with this theorist was Schubert. And he said, "Wouldn't that have killed Schubert as a composer?" You get the picture.

I used to be able to go to the piano and take out a book by Sechter called *The Correct Order of Fundamental Harmonies*.³ You must remember that Sechter, who seems very esoteric for you and very academic, was an enormous influence. His book was so successful, so important, that it was soon translated into English. This was an influential book, but all it consists of are series of chord progressions. Bruckner spent six years in his house studying with him. You can play Sechter harmony exercises and hear a kind of *Ursatz* of a Bruckner symphony. The effect of these theorists' "as ifs" was absolutely overwhelming, far more so than those of most theorists today. When Beethoven went to study with Albrechtsberger, the spats he had with him were on the order of "Why don't you like those parallel fifths?" There was no question in Beethoven's mind that Albrechtsberger was teaching him how music had to go. So the "as if" influence of these theorists (who were not really theorists, who were more pedagogues incorporating certain kinds of theoretical methodologies into their teaching) was absolutely overwhelming. So never assume that ours is the theoretical age. Ours is the theoretical age in the best sense of being much more sophisticated about what we think about saying about music. Take Fux for example. The formulation of the species was not Fux's; it was the outgrowth of a lot of such formulations. But he did not see the implications in the teaching of the species that were seen later by others, particularly Schenker.

Let's begin with the Schenker synthesis as it applies to Bach's C-Major

Chorale, #217. The achievement of Schenker is simply incredible, overwhelming, and therefore, if I were talking about him to a general public, I wouldn't say anything critical. But when we're sitting here together I'm perfectly willing to say anything about anybody. Schenker analysis was absolutely revolutionary back twenty-five years ago when I had to teach this kind of thing. Let me give you an idea about the atmosphere. When William Mitchell's harmony book came out in 1939, we used it at Princeton.[4] In the preface to that book he says that one can detect the influence of the ideas of Heinrich Schenker. In fact, the last chapter contains an analysis of Schumann's "Ich grolle nicht" from *Dichterliebe* which is sort of Schenkerian and doesn't have numbers under the chords but talks about lines. It's very mildly Schenkerian. If you look at the latest, third edition (1965), the name of Schenker is no longer in the preface, and this analysis is no longer there. So goes life. This is the reverse of what has really happened to Schenker, whose name was considered heretic in the thirties and is now hieratic in most places. But it is still somehow a volatile issue. I know of an institution regarded as a great university in which one of the composition teachers will not permit his students to go near anybody who mentions the name of Schenker.

Here are the first eight measures of Bach's Chorale #217, the simplest chorale I could find.

EXAMPLE 5-1

Let me tell you the story of this chorale as far as I'm concerned. When I was looking for a chorale to use in a very elementary harmony course many years ago, I came up with this one. The tune had absolutely no rhythmic complications, and Bach's harmonization of it has no complications: no chromatic complications to speak of, no complicated textures. It's the simplest chorale harmonization I could find which was really Bach. It comes out of Cantata 153. I must confess, I didn't quite discover this chorale. There was a composer named Nicholas Nabokov, whom you may have heard of because he wrote a couple of anecdotal books about music and he was a great friend of Stravinsky's. He was an international character in music and a fluent, if rather superficial, musician. In about 1936 we were talking about Bach chorales, and he said, "You know, I really worry about some of those Bach chorales. I wonder if it isn't dangerous to give them to students." At that time, the big new thing was to start harmony with a combination of counterpoint and Bach chorales. Ernest Bloch, who was Roger Sessions's teacher and therefore in a way my grand-teacher and someone whom I knew pretty well, always used nothing but Bach chorales to teach harmony. There were no great profundities in this, but it was the way things were going. Nicholas Nabokov said, "Bach really made a mistake with this chorale. It's absolutely wrong. Totally wrong. Bach's ear or something went wrong. He hit the wrong pedal or something."

This led me to use this chorale because it's a perfect example of how, on the one hand, a kind of Schenker memorative approach will lead you to end up exactly where Bach was. On the other hand, it suggests the things that a Schenker analysis may very well adumbrate but certainly not reveal. I don't want to spend too much time on this, but it's an aspect of Schenker which the Schenkerians would never talk about because it would seem somehow to downgrade their perfectly justified hero. And the rest of us don't write articles about these things.

Look at that chorale. The first thing that Nicholas Nabokov said was that Bach had absolutely the wrong harmony at this point (marked by an asterisk in example 5-1). I'd been using this chorale for years as the first chorale I ever looked at when one was beginning to deal with the rather larger-scale issues and more sophisticated questions than simply what chord to use at a certain spot and what note do you double. That is, looking at this as a predefined piece, it's a composition with certain kinds of compositional attributes; that's the way Bach saw it. From this viewpoint, what would you do with it to make it a four-part chorale? By a strange, incredible coincidence, this chorale was never mentioned anywhere in the literature until the Salzer/Schachter book came out.[5] Their book is a good one and very sophisticated; I would use it too, probably, if I felt obliged to use a textbook. Believe it or not, they came up with the same chorale, obviously for the same reasons I did, and it's all over their book. I agree with a great deal of their analysis and I agree that it leads to certain kinds of harmonic decisions. Unfortunately, they never point out that if you just analyze the piece this way, you're led to these decisions. And then they miss the boat. Forgive me, but they miss it terribly.

What harmony would you have under the A in measure 4? According to Nicholas Nabokov, any musician with a decent ear would use A minor. But if you really understood Schenker, you would say that you can't have a line going down from the D to the A and then have an A-minor triad. If you do that, you're not going to accomplish what seems the most obvious, but certainly not the only, interpretation of that piece, of having a preliminary line that goes C (m. 1), D (m. 3), D (m. 6), up to E (m. 9), at which point, to define that line, you'd certainly want to have a C in the bass (see ex. 5-3). This is real, practical Schenker, in the sense of hearing the piece as encompassing, taking in, prolonging, composing out a triad. If you're willing to take that point of view, the A minor is impossible because you get, in the most serious sense of the word, no enclosure by the C-major triad. Instead, you're composing out an A-minor triad; you're making the C in the bass in measure 1 the upper third of the A in measure 4. If you do that, you're getting structural parallel octaves. You don't ban them because you're not allowed to do parallel octaves; you ban them because of what happens to the C. It becomes the third of the A. If you really took in Schenker for what he revealed about the music of the past and the structure of tonal music, you couldn't possibly harmonize that with an A-minor triad. So what would you harmonize it with?

ANSWER: D major.

That's right, but if you don't know the chorale, if you've never heard it, it sounds weird. Taken by itself, it somehow doesn't sound right. It's probably not what somebody playing the piano by ear would arrive at at that point. From the point of view of hearing music in the small, you probably wouldn't choose that D-major triad. But there are also other contributory factors. You see, if you interpret Schenker in didactic terms (granted of course that you're working within a triadic system), you'd recognize the fact that once having eliminated that A–minor, you couldn't use a D-minor triad there either because of the B♮ in the previous measure. Therefore, it would have to be a D-major triad, and from a Schenkerian point of view, a lot of other things would also be determined on that D. As it turns out, they're all the things Bach did.

Let me be a historian of theory again for a moment. Do you know the relation between Bach and Rameau? When Rameau's theories began to be very widespread and were picked up in Germany by people such as Marpurg, Carl Philipp Emanuel Bach wrote a letter to Kirnberger saying, "My and my deceased father's basic principles are contrary to Rameau's."[6] The reason is obvious, of course. The idea of functional harmony chord progression was simply not the way he taught. Like Kirnberger, he approached chorale harmonization from the point of view of voice-leading figured-bass theory, which is from where so much of Schenker is alleged to come by Schenker himself. You would never, for example, arrive at this D-major triad on any kind of Rameau basis; again, I don't mean to be polemical.

Here are some other places where Schenker begins to get you synthetic Bachian details. What would you have in the alto voice under the D in measure 3? You would have an A, in order to make it perfectly clear that the upper-voice D was retained while you move into an inner voice and fill that space.

EXAMPLE 5-2

Things are being determined in this way that you could never get dropping out of functional harmony à la Rameau. Schenker's whole view of music immediately entails certain kinds of conclusions about musical progression—conclusions which could never be conjoined to the usual functional harmonic notion without simply adjoining a lot of new independent premises which would have no relationship to, and certainly not be entailed by, any of the other premises of functional harmony.

I'm not going to pretend what Bach does is inevitable, but we could reconstruct much of it. If you're going to make a connection between the C in measure 1 and the Ds in measure 3 and measure 6, which obviously you're going to do if you're going to think of this as the preliminary line moving up to the E, then it's quite clear what harmony you're going to have under the E in measure 9, isn't it? It has to be C major.

EXAMPLE 5-3

Another remarkable thing about this is something that would be almost redundant unless you have such a compositional notion in mind: the return under this third of G major (m. 7) of a G-major triad, which is, of course, a parallelism to what's going to happen to your treatment of the tonic triad in the large.

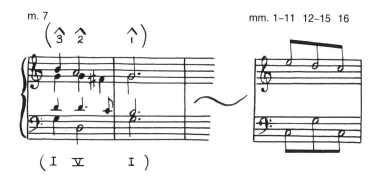

EXAMPLE 5-4

Here is another detail. The G in the alto in measure 6 makes it clear that the soprano G in measure 8 isn't the upper voice. The D in measure 6 is the upper voice; the soprano in measures 6–8 represents a movement into a middle voice.

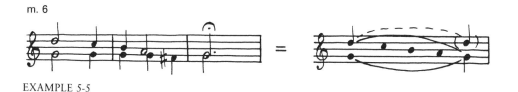

EXAMPLE 5-5

"Movement into an inner voice" and "retaining the upper voice" sound like such terribly abstract theoretical concepts. But after all, if you define the space between G and D in measure 6 and then move into it, the G has already been stated as an inner voice. It doesn't add anything new such as the upper-voice D does when it's treated as it is in measure 6.

What I really want to get on to is what happens next in measure 9. I'm being summary, but the details are easily filled in by nothing more than the same sort of presumptions of attitude. When you get to measure 9, hell breaks loose. Now I'd like someone who is devoted to the principles of the Piston harmony book[7] to tell me what to do next.

EXAMPLE 5-6

This is where Salzer and Schachter really have problems. The next thing that Bach does violates three rules of every harmony book that was ever written. What would you do if you were harmonizing measure 9? Look at the things that are conjoined in this tiny little modest composition that might provide you with the criteria for harmonization, for progression, for movement. We've already established that on the first beat of measure 9, when you've reached scale-degree three, you support it with your tonic. That's where your line has come from. You've superimposed the E over the C now, and the C is going to appear in the soprano in the next measure quite literally. How would you treat the second and third beats? Think like a composer, not like you're doing a harmony exercise. Bach was given this chorale. He probably said, "What a rotten tune but I'll do my best with it." What did he do? I defy anybody here who doesn't know the chorale to guess what Bach did and I don't mean to pretend for a moment that I would have done it. Salzer and Schachter certainly would never have done it. The next two beats are all I want. The next three beats if you wish.

ANSWER: Well, you can't respace the C chord there as well as you could if the root were in the soprano. With the E in the soprano, you don't want to double it in the bass.

Why can't you double an E? I think doubled Es are sometimes lovely. The rule that's going to be violated now is so much worse than doubling the third that you might want to flunk Bach. Give me the next note. Tell me what you would do as dynamic creative personalities.

ANSWER: Well, how about a descending bass line C–B–A.

Okay, why not? It's one of those things that anybody might do who's been around, playing a little double bass pizzicato with a little walking bass à la Irving Berlin. But why do you want C–B–A there? What would it get you? What happens here so clearly comes out of the piece. And you let him do it even though it violates some notion of rules that you've inhibitedly inherited from, as my friend Schenker would say, false teaching.

What's the next step? Remember, this is a simple chorale; this is not one of those complicated chorales that Berg would have used. How about a G♯ in the bass? How about a G♯ which does all kinds of terrible things, gives you a false relation, gives you a dissonant leap in the bass, and then, why not just cross a few voices, which you're not supposed to do, while you're at it? Three wrongs make a right. You said he couldn't parallel the beginning but he does parallel the beginning. After having established the tonal basis of the E on beat 1 of measure 9, the triadic basis, that's exactly what he does. He motivically parallels the opening. And if you don't pay any attention to the motivic (or, if you wish, linear) parallelism, then obviously you're not going to come up with an answer.

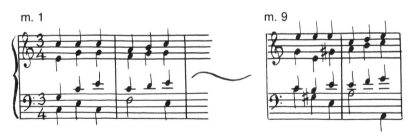

EXAMPLE 5-7

Almost every Bach chorale has something like this (ex. 5-7). As a student you're told, "This is a license and if you're a genius you're allowed to do these things, but please, in your own work, no false relations, no crossed voices, no dissonances in the bass or anywhere else."

From this point, the piece goes on with all kinds of parallelisms.

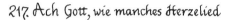

EXAMPLE 5-8

The fermata harmonies in the first half, V/V to V, are paralleled in the second half by V to I. The F and F♯ in the bass in measures 14 and 15 parallel the F–F♯ you had back in measures 2 and 3. The only dissonance that you get in the second half you could probably guess by now. It's that second resolving down in measure 14, which is exactly parallel with the dissonance in measure 7. That second is formed by the second degree in measure 14; in measure 7 it involves the second degree within the tonicization of G. The third is always associated with a root position triad; it is so associated in measure 7 within G major, and again in measure 13. That's all I really want to do with this.

This is the simplest example I know of what Schenker gets you and then what Schenker doesn't get you. He obviously doesn't get you very far towards these kinds of structural relations or towards parallelisms in particular. When Salzer and Schachter get to measure 9, they say, "By using cross-relations, we make the texture less smooth. Smoothness, however, is by no means a constant requirement; and to forbid cross-relations at this stage would be sheer pedantry."[8] Now at what stage do you stop forbidding false relations because they become sheer pedantry? They introduce the notion of smoothness, but they don't tell you why Bach doesn't use smoothness there and uses it somewhere else or in some other piece. They say, "The cross-relation results from the sudden climactic use of high register underscoring the appearance of the tonic C in the bass."[9] What they're saying is that two wrongs make a right. The logic breaks down completely because they just don't pay any attention to this parallelism. This is exactly the kind of thing that you often miss in Schenker: explicit discussion of motivic parallelism and the way in which a parallelism will induce parallelisms in other dimensions. All I'm interested in is showing you the fact that conventional theory will simply not work.

QUESTION: Can you underscore again what the parallelism is between measures 1–2 and measures 9–10?

Just this—it's just literal. First you get the tonic—a result of the preliminary line—then on beat 2 you get the first inversion. The harmonies on the second and third beats of measure 9 are exactly the same with regard to E as those in measure 1 are with the C, literally the same harmonies, same relation. The structures are literally identical and then go up to exactly the same place. In measure 2 it gets you an F-major triad. In measure 10 it gets you an A-minor triad, all by virtue of the same bass movement. In order to get that parallelism, he has to use a G♯. He can't use a G♮, because it won't function as a local leading tone. This is not supposed to be a virtuoso trick. This is the kind of thing that is supposed to show what Schenker does give you that you don't get otherwise, as with old-fashioned conventional harmony of the kind that I was brought up on. If you got to a place like measure 4, conventional harmony wouldn't give you the sense of looking ahead. You would decide only what's possible locally.

Remember, by the way, that the notion of secondary sevenths, or applied dominants or whatever word you're taught to use, is already a very sophisticated notion, something that came in with Riemann. Riemann is woefully inadequate, obviously, in terms of what we would like to see an analysis do. Riemann pays no attention whatsoever to any kind of voice leading. His analysis is like the worst kind of, not figured-bass analysis, but functional harmony analysis. Anything can go anywhere; it makes no difference whatsoever. All you look at is the collection which he calls the harmony. His approach would yield none of what we found in the chorale.

On the other hand, Riemann's impulse was obviously in the direction in which theory was going. Instead of talking about moving from a G-major triad to a B-major triad or moving from the first theme in E♭ to the second theme in B♭, he was talking about areas. There's a very interesting book by Hermann Erpf, a devout Riemann disciple, called *Studien zur Harmonie und Klangtechnik der neueren Musik*.[10] It begins with Beethoven and includes an analysis of the slow movement of the *Waldstein*. I refer to it because *Readings in Schenker Analysis*, Maury Yeston's collection, contains a symposium on the slow movement of the *Waldstein*.[11] There's a very conventional Schenkerian analysis by David Beach, which has an interesting aspect: its strong language.[12] You know the kind of violent language that Schenkerians use with regard to each other. If you've ever read Ernst Oster's comments on Roy Travis, you know what I mean.[13] It becomes violent, really violent. David Beach simply says that Felix Salzer's analysis of the B♭ in measure 6 is a mistake.[14]

Now, what makes a mistake? One could assume either that Salzer has misinterpreted Schenker and therefore it's not a good Schenker analysis—which interests me about as little as anything in the world—or that his is simply a mistaken way to view the piece, which interests me very much. You see one of my problems with many books on Schenker analysis is that they teach you how to make a Schenker graph but not how to understand a piece of music. I'm not very much interested in learning how to make Schenker graphs, and this is not to belittle Schenker (I don't have to say that ever again, I trust).

Here is the Erpf analysis[15] of the famous beginning of that famous movement.

Anhang: Analyse ausgewählter Musikbeispiele.

Musikbeispiel Nr. 9: Beethoven, Sonate op. 53, 2. Satz, Takt 1—9.

EXAMPLE 5-9

Let me tell you what Erpf does. He begins by saying that Riemann is obviously his model. At the beginning he has a series of what he calls function relations. It looks almost exactly like the functional table in the Schoenberg *Structural Functions*.[16] He says that Riemann was obviously right, that music really consists of defined regions, that you don't need to worry about individual chords, you only see how they contribute to a large region, but that he's going to forget this stuff of Riemann's about parallel undertone series with minor triads being the major triad in the undertone. Indeed, he says there are only two regions in music: the tonic and the dominant. The subdominant, for him (though he would often view this contextually), turns up as the relative major of the second degree. What is terribly interesting is that he does analyses like the one in example 5-9. That's a very problematical passage. Erpf began doing what was a commonplace in my day. Forgive me for saying "in my day" but you may never have encountered this. Have you encountered anybody who says that all music is really tonal, and therefore, if you start a piece with a chord like example 5-10, then that chord is obviously a dominant with a neurotic thirteenth and a vagrant seventh, and everything is analyzable?

EXAMPLE 5-10

The funny part about Erpf is that he started analyzing other, later music and it took him a little further forward. He got to the Liszt *Faust Symphony*, and he said, "It doesn't make any sense any longer to put these functional indications under these harmonies. It's not telling me the things about the music that seem most pertinent about the music." So he began categorizing things in remarkable ways, in terms of symmetrical chords, for example, in the *Faust Symphony*. It's a remarkable historical example. (By the way, the *Faust Symphony* is a twelve-tone piece as you obviously can see! Four augmented triads chromatically related will give you a twelve-tone thingy-dingy! See ex. 5-11.)

EXAMPLE 5-11

But Erpf didn't say that. He said, "These are symmetrical chords and the symmetry has much more to do with the internal redundancy than anything I might call them." Little by little, he comes to the conclusion that he has to analyze these things from a contextual point of view.

Riemann's analysis of the *Waldstein* uses a notation that combines functional harmony with voice-leading alteration technique but exhibits no concern whatsoever for actual linear events. You see, it's amazing to anybody's ear, except perhaps to someone who's been so indoctrinated, that the bass could be altered from its actual chromatic descent to the shape it takes in example 5-12b without affecting the analysis.

EXAMPLE 5-12

As far as the Riemann analysis is concerned, either way the bass had gone, it would have been the same analysis. This strikes many of us as being rather an unreal way of viewing a piece of music—in terms of the characteristics which are likely to be used in the piece. He completely disregards the chromatic motion in the bass. But I just wanted to tell you about Mr. Erpf and his analysis.

The very first of the sketches in Schenker's *Five Graphic Analyses* is a Bach chorale.[17] This analysis is for me an incredible example of the kind of thing that Schenker did point out, at least by strong implication, and never followed up on. The interesting thing about this is that it's in many ways like that earlier chorale, but the parallelism occurs in a different way. The parallelism here has to do with the two sections (I don't want to say *phrases,* a word that, because of its ambiguity, I never use). There are two parallel sections of the piece. And I'm going just to assume the Schenker analysis whether you agree with it or not. The idea of Schenker as synthesis is what I'm trying to get at.

117. *Nun ruhen alle Wälder*

EXAMPLE 5-13

Can you imagine any criterion in the world that could be gleaned from traditional harmony (by which I mean traditional, basically Rameau-based harmony, not figured-bass harmony) which could explain why you shouldn't have a nice root position triad to harmonize the Ab in measure 5? Is there any rule of harmony you know that forbids that as it forbids parallel fifths (nasty sounds)? But if you were viewing this from the Schenker point of view, you simply could not have a root position triad with that A♭. And in the ten harmonizations that Bach makes of this chorale there's never a root position triad under that A♭. There can't be because the line would end at that point. That's the kind of thing that I would regard as a little more reasonable basis for teaching what is in some places called harmony. From the C before measure 1 to the C in measure 2 under the fermata, you maintain that constancy, the A♭ in the bass. The B♭ in measure 3 is harmonized by the dominant which recurs under the fermata in measure 4. At the A♭ in measure 5 you *have* to have at least something as weak as that because otherwise your ear would take you C, B♭, A♭, and the piece from any musical point of view is over. What does it mean for a piece to be over? Not just that you repeat fourteen C-major triads and then everybody yells "bravo."

The details are perfectly clear. It's quite obvious that the D♭ against C becomes a feature of the piece very early in the game and it's constantly reinforced. This feature is in the Schenker sketch, but he doesn't draw attention to it the way he does, for example, to the C against A♭. Even with this in mind, who wouldn't use a nice six-four chord under the third-to-last note? If you look around in this piece to find out where that major seventh root position occurs, you notice that it's exactly the same collection that you had on the first beat of measure 2, and that he constantly reiterates the D♭–C association. It takes you back to the beginning. It's a harmony that's generated by internal relationships, rather than by a general rule by which you'd get to a six-four.

If you look at Schenker's analysis, you recognize two things. In the whole section following the third fermata, since Bach does not harmonize it the same way as he did the first time, now you get an E♮ in the bass in measure 6. Now the whole section from measure 7 through the downbeat of measure 11 is a great big passing note. Schenker makes the very good point that the F in the bass is the sixth degree, a passing note. This is similar, in some ways, to that point in Schenker's analysis of the *Eroica* Symphony where he describes most of the development section of the first movement as a big neighbor note. He has a B♭ (the dominant) for the so-called second theme and then shows motion up through a B♮ to C. The C is a big neighbor note, following which you go down through C♭ and back to B♭ and then to the recapitulation.

Everyone's heard the famous story about Schoenberg and this analysis by Schenker. It was alleged that somebody showed it to Schoenberg. Now God knows what that means. The analysis is enormous—you could spread it all over this building. Probably the story refers to just the first page of the analysis, just the most "ur" of the *Ursätze*. Schoenberg is alleged to have said, "But where are my favorite places?"

First of all, I am assured by people who should know (like Leonard Stein) that this story is totally apocryphal. Schoenberg had probably studied the *Eroica* analysis long before anybody around UCLA had shown it to him (even if they dared do such a thing). But I like the story because I would like to have thought that it was true and that I was there. Because if someone asked, "Where are my favorite places?" you could answer, "Well, would those places be your favorites in *Scheherazade*? Would they be your favorite places if they popped up in the middle of *The Merry Widow*? They're your favorite places in a great big piece called the *Eroica* Symphony. They're your favorite places, we hope, because they're part of the continuity and part of the context, and who provides a better characterization of this continuity and context than does Schenker?"

I'm not at all unsure of the fact that one of the reasons that Schoenberg made his devastating statement about the music of his middle period—that he couldn't write music of sufficient complexity or great enough length—was because he did look at such things as the Schenker. We know he did because he always put Schenker at the top of his lists of books that should be studied in school. He may have looked at Schenker's *Eroica* analysis and seen that big neighboring note. He may have thought, "How in the devil can one create such huge sections which in some sense can be unified by some kind of functionality or centricity if you don't have tonality?" That's what Schoenberg meant by "sufficient complexity and great enough length." He didn't mean number of notes per square inch, obviously—just look at *Erwartung*! He means structural complexity.

Now let's get back to the chorale itself. The dominant of VI occurs under the fifth fermata just as the dominant of I occurred under the second fermata. That's a parallelism. Notice the neat relation between this parallelism and the parallelism in the C-Major Chorale. There, the melody was sequentially repeated so you used the parallelism of holding the relation fixed. Here the notes are repeated so you've got a different kind of parallelism, a functional parallelism. Indeed V of VI at the fifth fermata is the only dominant-tonic relationship you could possibly have within this idiom that would parallel the V of I at the second fermata. Try anything else and it won't work. This works.

Now what do you do to continue that parallelism? You violate all the rules of harmony. What are you going to put under the G in measure 10? You can hear it practically in the overtone series. There's only one thing you can do. Put in an E♮. You put in an E♮ and look what you've got: an E♭ following it in exactly the same register. You've got a terrible false relation or chromaticism. Now what would you do? To where would you go back and make that a feature of the piece; how would you do it?

ANSWER: How about an A♮ under the previous fermata?

Good. Now, be very inventive. Just imagine that you, like Bach, had a friend named Lorenz Mizler who is very imaginative and who said, "Bach, you know you really gotta break your little baroque binds here. Think about music like a composer; I mean, you know, you're not Vivaldi after all—you can really write music." See, this for me is a composer-written work. By the way, Schenker has not said any of this. Let's just make it clear I take full responsibility for everything after this. Schenker does make it clear that there are these parallel lines, parallel functionality. He didn't say anything about D♭'s and C's. That's not his schtick. (Notice right there with the first chord in measure 7, the F under the A♭, the tenor figuration reminds you of the C–D♭ that he began the piece with, but that's just an added plus there.)

Back to the fourth fermata. What's the next chord going to be?

ANSWER: The A will move to A♭.

Good. If you were doing conventional harmony, how could you ever come up with an F-major triad at the fermata, then immediately switch to an F-minor triad? What could possibly be the motivation? The chorale melody in measure 10 forced you into this E–E♭, and now you make that a feature of the piece by going A–A♭ in measure 8. Can you find any explanation within the bounds of so-called traditional harmony that could possibly suggest this except again the implication, well, that this was a genius? Some critics will suddenly pull that twist on you.

I have only one last thing to offer. Right after the fifth fermata, we go to an A♭ in the melody. One thing we certainly know is we're not going to have a tonic triad under that A♭, right? Impossible. That's coming at the end. We're not going to end the piece here; the piece ends over there at the end. We're not Dvořák either. Do you know that place in the Cello Concerto where everyone applauds prematurely? It's a wonderful example of what people listen to in music. They hear a root position triad (even though it's not the tonic), and they all start applauding. Now back to Bach. What would you do under the Ab? It's a question of the kinds of things one can get from Schenker without literally getting them from Schenker. I don't know any other approach that would have gotten us into this. You could perhaps have seen the parallelism of this in the cadences, but now consider it quite detached from the motivation of the tonal parallelism. (I'm not going to worry about the chord immediately after the fermata. We know it has to be a C-minor triad for the parallelism, and that's exactly what it is. He doesn't pull any punches with that at all.)

Now where do you go next? You can't do what you did at the analogous spot in measure 4, because this is a different cup of tea. There's a different relationship between the outer voices. Where would you go? I wonder how anybody in those days except Bach might have come up with this particular little stroke. What would you do? Suppose you're taking a Prix de Rome examination. They've got you locked in a room. Do you want never to come out? What do we do?

ANSWER: How about an F-minor triad?

All right, you're coming. I guess that would be possible.

ANSWER: How about Db in the first inversion?

All right. Not great. Not terrible. Neither is impossible. But it's not a matter of which of these is possible or acceptable, rather that there's one which is a real stroke.

Think about the dual function of those two passages, just think about them. They were made as parallel as two passages can be. The first was involved with the tonic; the second has been involved with VI. Why don't you just do something real cute? How about combining the two triads into one fell swoop and getting both triads reflecting both of those parallel sections? And if somebody says, "We all know what that is. That's just a VI7," you can say "Why there?" From here on in, it's easy. You'll recognize, by the way, that some of these harmonies coming up are things you heard earlier, we just can't go into all of that. And then you're through. You get the C over the

A♭ again in measure 11. You get a summing up of the whole harmonic process and a last C–D♭ at the end.

I don't know how long it took Bach to harmonize this, but I can assure you this is not the first time that I've done this. I saw these sketches of Schenker when they were first issued by Hans Weisse at the Mannes School, long before they were published by Dover. They were the first things really available of that kind in English. And therefore, I used them with classes way back. There is nothing else like this chorale anywhere. What I suspect is that if any other composer did anything this far out and imaginative, the music was probably swept out when he died and we never heard about it, which is probably where most of the best music is.

I'm going to shift the subject quite radically now. Any of you who are interested can look in Yeston's *Readings in Schenker Analysis* for analyses of the *Waldstein* by Beach and others. The one by David Beach is particularly interesting not only to compare with the Erpf generally but because of the contention between the two as to how one interprets a certain note. Ask yourself what the different analyses would do to a performance of the piece. That's the interesting thing. This is a very difficult piece to play. I don't mean technically; most of us can get through it; but it's still a very difficult piece to play. And the question of how your conception of where that B♭ in measure 6 came from, and how it functioned in that big overall line, would tell you a great deal about how you'd shape the passage. And that is obviously very interesting.

Apropos performance, consider the clarinet line of the opening of the slow movement of the Mozart Clarinet Quintet.

EXAMPLE 5-14

This is not my analysis; this is one that was noticed by people long before I did anything except play the clarinet. As you look at that simple little melody, do you notice anything internal about it that might suggest to you how you as a performer might do something with the piece?

What would you notice about this that might influence the way you would breathe if you were a clarinetist, or the way you would phrase? It's as good an example to me as my example of those second six notes in the first set statement of the Schoenberg Fourth Quartet: the way people are simply not prepared to hear those six notes as arranged in space. This is an example of what you might hear first in a piece when there are other things that other people would hear first. Do you notice anything about this, any internal things that might suggest to you something worth remarking?

ANSWER: The tones in the upper register form a line—F♯ to G to F♯.

You're being too sophisticated. If this were something so wildly esoteric and recondite that I had to pull numbers out of my hat or indulge in what was once politely called "note-picking," that would be something else. But that's not it. Here's what it is: a simple parallelism of a striking kind. Sequential repetition (see brackets in example 5-14). Nobody heard that.

My ego is less than involved in this. Although it seemed perfectly obvious to me, it's not mine—you just go out and read *Dreiklang* and there it is.[18] A man once became very enraged when I pointed this out. He's a musicologist and they have a tendency to get enraged when theorists or composers talk. He said, "I've been playing the clarinet all my life and I played that piece at least a hundred times and I never noticed it." Now, my response could have been, "What did you ever notice in a piece?" I didn't say that. I simply regard this as another interesting phenomenon.

Obviously we're much more accustomed to hearing what I call "sweet-and-sour" beats rather than hearing the pitches as they unfold. You are obviously being taken in by the fact that the A is the beginning of a two-measure what's-it and the E is the beginning of another two-measure what's-it. But if you look at it from that point of view, things disappear. Now, therefore, as a clarinetist would you like to suggest by some sort of subtle articulation that you're beginning across the bar line? The idea that music is somehow concerned to present the strong beat is something that I've never understood. I leave that to, again, the sweet-and-sour beat lovers. This seems to me a much more subtle way of performing the piece and of construing the piece.

When you begin with this, you begin with real Schenker. For me, diminution technique is the essence of Schenker. I don't mean it's the only thing, but I don't usually use the word *essence*. I doubt if anybody's ever heard me use the word *essence* before, but what I simply mean by it is the most valuable aspects of Schenker's work, in which he demonstrates the way in which a piece can indeed induce this kind of successive subsumption which I think is absolutely necessary. For me, the remarkable aspect of Schenker is what it tells you about musical memory and the way in which you can take in a piece, because obviously you can't take in a passage unless you chunk it and relate it and parallel it in a variety of ways. I think that his is a most efficient description of this process. For all that it is, I think I've also indicated that it's an incomplete description as far as I'm concerned. I'm sure you've seen many other parallelisms and things of this kind in the Burkhart article and other places.[19]

The thing that's remarkable about this is that this is the way Mozart taught. That's the thing that I find fascinating. What Schenker called diminution was basic to instruction in music in Germany and England. In England it was called the theory of divisions.[20] For example, Purcell, in his "Brief Introduction to the Art of Descant," shows how he harmonizes something.[21] It has nothing to do with anything you ever talk about when you do functional harmony. Now, Purcell's name coming from me you might regard as strange. (It'd be stranger if you heard Purcell's music coming from me!) Purcell turns out to be a guy who really thought about these issues. If you can penetrate his terminology, which is very British (who can compute a crotchet?), you will find it's extraordinary the way he chooses pitches. He takes a melody and tells you certain notes with which he chooses to harmonize it on the basis of quite familiar tonal techniques. Then he tells you why he will not choose a certain note here because of redundancy, another one here because of intervallic repetition. Incredible! The criteria have nothing to do with Rameau's criteria whatsoever, absolutely nothing. And the thing is, that's what Mozart would teach his students. Above all, there was a famous English student whose lessons with Mozart have been talked about a great deal.[22] The notion of divisions is the kind of thing they would teach.

There's a very funny instance of this in Mattheson's *The Well-tempered Kapellmeister,* in which the Kapellmeister-with-qualities tells you how to write a piece.[23] You're sitting home one night, you've got a commission, you've got to write a piece, you haven't got an idea, so you take somebody else's tune and, by having a real control of the practice of divisions, you ornament it in such a way that nobody would ever recognize it. You take a fundamental thing and you elaborate it. In other words, you employ diminution technique, in other words, divisions. And in Mozart's teaching, often of very sophisticated students, this is, of course, one of the absolutely fundamental criteria: that is, how you create parallelisms, how you make the parallelism contrapuntal, how you create polyphonic contrapuntalisms, if you wish. That Mozart would do this is only an example to show that this was a technique that he was constantly not only espousing but teaching, one that was considered part of the fundamental technique. When you did counterpoint, you did theory of divisions with it.

It's like dear old Brahms. Brahms demanded that all of his sketches be destroyed at his death, as you probably know, and most of them were. But every morning he would get up, and the way some of you go jogging or bicycling or whatever you do, his exercise would be to start with a first-species measure and he'd start expanding and expanding and expanding à la Peter Westergaard.[24] And he would get a hunk of a piece. Sometimes he would use these hunks for some of his choral music, and sometimes he just wanted to see what would come out if he started in a different way and began again elaborating and elaborating according to species counterpoint.

Let's lead into associative harmony and middle Schoenberg and so forth (none of that sophisticated twelve-tone stuff) by way of the *Tristan* Prelude. My favorite comment on the *Tristan* Prelude was that of my friend Mr. Stettenheim, who said that it was a "wild chaos of tones."[25] That was about fifteen years after the piece was first performed, and he thought it sounded like a wild chaos of tones, which is perfectly understandable. About another quarter of a century after that, the famous composer/theorist Salomon Jadassohn made a similar comment. Mr. Jadassohn was the chief teacher of composition and everything else at the Leipzig Conservatory. He wrote books on canon and fugue, form, and everything else you could think of, and he wrote a book entirely devoted to the melody and harmony of Wagner.[26] He said that any fool will see how this *Tristan* Prelude goes: it simply passes through fourteen keys in the first twelve measures. This for him was an explication in terms of the received normal theory of his time. Once you can locate things in tonalities, a piece was explicated and therefore satisfactory and therefore, I assume, a coherent piece of music. Now his explication may seem to many of you a representation of chaos rather than of coherence. The fact of the matter is that it was satisfactory for him.

This is a big theoretical issue. What constitutes a sufficient explanation? What's a satisfactory explanation? What about the scope of an explanation?

But what was remarkable was just as you did not see the diminution in the Mozart Clarinet Quintet, and just as most do not hear that inversion in space of a mere hexachord in Schoenberg's Fourth Quartet, nobody apparently noticed any of the parallelisms with which Wagner was working. There are composers, whose names are simply no longer known for many reasons (they went down the drain), who come out of this tradition, who used these techniques, extended them for what superficially would sound like a much more advanced music, a much more complex music, a much more chromatic music, who *did* infer these things. They didn't write about them, however. If they discovered these things, they weren't going to write an article. First of all, there were no places to write articles. There was no *Music Theory Spectrum* or even *Musical Quarterly*. And they weren't going to give away these secrets. These things were going to be the basis for their techniques. So, while the Jadassohns, who were sort of official composers who didn't write this way but who wrote theory books, were talking about the fourteen different keys in the first twelve measures, these people were hearing other things.

People have had absurd arguments about the opening of this piece.

EXAMPLE 5-15

Is the A in measure 2 a passing note or does the G♯ resolve to the A? Is the G♯ really the accented dissonance or appoggiatura, and is the chord in measure 2 really formed with the A? Therefore, is it really a subdominant or is it really a dominant, or how high is up? But questions like that require you to fit the piece into some received theory, which is what Jadassohn did. As Jadassohn pointed out, the chord at the beginning of measure 2 is the leading tone seventh in F♯, so what are you getting excited about? The piece is in F♯ for the first chord. It's only there for the first chord, but isn't F♯ good enough to be in for part of a measure? And so it went and so the whole thing went. The remarkable part about this whole opening of the Prelude, and the whole Prelude, is how it became a source of various ways of functioning. The reason I'm bringing it up now is because I think the next piece we'll go on to will be the Schoenberg, Opus 16, Number 3, which uses exactly the same technique. Of course, Schoenberg knew *Tristan* full well. Everybody knew this piece cold: it was their *Melancholy Baby*. Just in the first three measures, things are already beginning to develop. One can talk about all the means of continuity. Just picking up the same pitch class and taking it from there is more like Webern than any composer that was around in those days. Just the idea of picking up and making the last first—using such a continuity, even if it's a somewhat simple-minded continuity. The upper voice goes from G♯ up to B, and then B up to D, then from D up to F♯, always through a very limited supply of sonorities. (Did you ever hear the Furtwängler recording? The piano doesn't live that long. That's the way people played it, even slower than that.) The B in measure 6 is now harmonized by D, F♯, and A♭. From one point of view this is nothing but a transposition of the first chord through a minor third, but what is more, it's the central one of the three Tristan chords (mm. 2, 6, and 10). As the central one, it contains G♯, B, D, and F♯, just as the upper line moves from G♯ to B, B to D, and D to F♯. That seems to me to be already a kind of association that's a little stronger than worrying about whether you're really in F or really in A or what is "really," or whether these dominant seventh chords would indicate anything if they had gone to their appointed rounds on their appointed rounds, which, of course, they never do.

But, getting back to this associative harmony, what would you want to say in a purely contextual sense about this harmonic progression? In fact, there are a lot of similar things that are remarkable throughout this whole opera. Have any of you ever read Lorenz's analysis of *Tristan*? Alfred Lorenz did analyses of all the big Wagner operas in four volumes—one for *Tristan*, one for *Meistersinger*, one for *Parsifal*, and one for the *Ring*—in which he finds incredible parallelisms.[27] He shows that *Tristan*, for example, is laid out with libretto parallelisms of a remarkable kind. The opera begins with Brangena and Isolde. In the third act, everything is paralleled. What Brangena is to Isolde in the first act, Kurvenal is to Tristan in the third act. The first act opens with the unaccompanied sailor song; the third act opens with a closely related unaccompanied English horn solo. The same lines are stuck in different contexts throughout. These are very carefully worked out libretti, and much of the parallelism is reflected in the music. The Tristan chord appears exactly as a Tristan chord something like 1,400 times in the opera (Lorenz counted them).

What makes it the Tristan chord? Do you notice any characteristic about it as a chord that's worth noticing? (Some people say it's half-diminished, although I don't understand their arithmetic; to me, it seems it's at least three-quarters diminished.) Of the six intervals involved, none is repeated. It is similar to the chord in Strauss's *Till Eulenspiegel*, but Strauss uses it in a different way. Strauss repeats the interval of 3—let's use chromatic notation here because there's no sense talking about major or minor thirds or any of that—B♭ to D♭ to E.

EXAMPLE 5-16

Wagner sets it up so that there's a unique interval between any two notes, so you have a packet of unique intervals which he uses to define spaces in the piece. The Tristan chord is laid out so you have the intervals 6, 10, 3, 4, 9, 5. That layout is crucial to the way this chord is used in the piece, and, of course, it has the same intervals in all of its repetitions. You can also view it as a fourth with a tritone a major third away. The next chord, formed with the A in measure 2, consists of two tritones: A–D♯ and B–F. The next chord, on the first beat of measure 3, also consists of two tritones (A♯–E and D–G♯) and thus has the same structure as the previous one, although it's not at all obvious. (Maybe if you played it as slowly as Furtwängler does, you'd become accustomed to the sonorities.) What is this next chord (end of measure 3)? Well, everybody said, "Anybody can tell what that is—that's a good old dominant seventh." Well, what's the good old dominant seventh? The good old dominant seventh is intervallically the same chord as the first one—it's the Tristan chord! So, you see, you don't have to think of this as being a functional dominant seventh unless you insist that whenever you hear a dominant seventh (as you do in measure 2 of Schoenberg's Opus 33a), it necessarily functions as a dominant seventh.

Basically, you have a symmetrical pattern whereby the outer two chords and the inner two chords are intervallically the same.

EXAMPLE 5-17

They're simply transposed inversions and nothing but. It's like Schoenberg's Opus 33a—the same kind of pattern. This is real associative harmony. These harmonies are related to one another in a particular way and distributed in such a way that if some of them happen to come out sounding like familiar dominant sevenths (which I'm sure Wagner did intend in some sense), nevertheless you now have a string of them. And, equally fascinating, the highest voice goes G♯ to B, and B to D, but when you get up to D and expect to go to F, he goes instead to F♯. His line thus outlines the Tristan chord, and he ends up at F♯ by means of a composed-out accelerando, which is exactly what you get in the Schoenberg Opus 16, Number 3.

There's a remarkable thing that Wagner does throughout this whole piece that Stravinsky—I can't believe that he knew this—came up with as a way to make connections, purely contextual contingencies and dependencies. When Wagner gets to the last of the chords (m. 11), he's filling in a *major* third (D–F♯) in the upper voice, not just a minor third as he did before. Now notice that in an inner voice he replicates a progression that you already know. Starting in measure 10, the bassoon, in that middle voice, has F–E–D♯. Now the bassoon doesn't play for quite a few measures, but what's the next note in the bassoon going to have to be?

ANSWER: D♮.

Of course, D♮. The bassoon stops playing in measure 11 with a D♯. When it comes in again in measure 16, it has to have a D♮. He's simply setting up these contingencies which, of course, relate to the very first notes you heard in the piece but now operate in a completely different context.

EXAMPLE 5-18

And so it goes.

There's one other thing perhaps I should say. The *Tristan* Prelude ends in a way which really clinches it for anybody who wants to talk about Wagner and the future of music. In the unaccompanied double basses, the Tristan chord appears at the original level (Eb–B–F–Ab) but linearized.

EXAMPLE 5-19

If you think this is too rudimentary and not worthy of your attention, try the prelude to the third act of *Parsifal*! The prelude to the third act of *Parsifal* is one of the most mysterious pieces ever written, and I don't mean just in this kind of remarkable detail. Certain things pop out immediately. It's a highly contrapuntal piece which begins with a sort of canon by inversion. It's not even clear as to why he changed the key signature in the places he did. It just isn't clear what's going on there at all, even in the mechanical externals. It's a very difficult piece to hear through.

Apropos of difficult pieces to hear through, I'll tell you one of my Schenker anecdotes. Many years ago, I was dealing with one of the really expert Schenkerians; indeed, it was Ernst Oster. Ernst was a dyed-in-the-wool Schenkerian, by which I mean he knew the stuff cold. He was a wonderful musician. He would scream for hours at you as to how you should interpret a particular Ab in a particular piece. He knew ten times as much of the literature as all of us put together because he did nothing else except the literature. He didn't compose and he didn't read about anything else—this was his world and life. One day I said, "Ernst, why has no Schenkerian ever done an analysis of a Brahms piece? Now I know the Brahms *Handel Variations* analysis. It's an early piece and a trivial analysis. But what about the Third

Symphony or the G-Minor Quintet, one of the big pieces." He said, "They're too difficult." So I said, "Well, if they're too difficult for you to analyze, how do you know they're any good?"

You must remember that Schenker said that Brahms was the last great master of German music. This was a great problem for them. It stuck them very much because they really couldn't handle Brahms. There is no published analysis of Brahms in Schenker except for the *Handel Variations* analysis, which is okay, but that's a variation piece and an early piece. If any of you have lived with, let's say, the Third Symphony (just to take one example), not to mention the Clarinet Quintet, you know that these pieces really are quite difficult from the Schenkerian point of view. You would always think that you didn't have a handle on them because, every time you went back to them, you found things that you'd never noticed before. Of course, as a composer, you realize that it's possible to go back to your own pieces and notice things which you've never noticed before, things which now seem to you of a possible significance.

I got so bored with the history of theory that I started dealing with all the idiosyncratic things and all the crazy people, people like Reicha. But even these people could be extremely influential. When Berlioz went to the French Conservatory, he loved Reicha. He thought all the other people were very boring, but Reicha he liked because Reicha was sort of a nut. Full of ideas that didn't pan out. If you were a woodwind player, you'd say, "Reicha? He wrote all those very dull conservatory pieces." But those were pieces that he wrote for examinations at the conservatory: they had nothing to do with his real composition; they were just his bread and butter. He was an absolute madman who had ideas of how to compose that changed from day to day. If any of you are, by the way, interested in French opera, he wrote an incredible series of volumes on how to write a French opera, in which he just told you how to do the things that were regarded as the acceptable things to do when you wrote French opera.[28] If you're not interested, don't read it, because it's very hard to get through; you have to know a lot of French and you have to know a lot of French opera. (And there's nothing I wouldn't do to avoid that.) But he's one of the crazy men, and he was interesting.

Abt Vogler is another eccentric figure who is worth talking about apropos Bach chorales and such things. The effect of Abt Vogler would be considered to be one of these absolutely peripheral insanities if you didn't stop and bother to find out about the composers who adored him, who believed that he was giving them the absolute hallowed word, and who therefore were tremendously influenced by him.

Let's return for a moment to Erpf. I want to show you a few little characteristic things. He talks about *Kette,* which is a term that you probably never heard. It describes a situation in which, according to the analysis, the tonality seems neutralized. You get just chains of things so that you're no longer contained within a particular collection, a tonality collection, but rather within just a simple chromatic chain, and so, therefore, a tonal nomenclature no longer makes any sense. Of course, the *Tristan* Prelude could be described in this way. And for the *Tristan* Prelude, Erpf no longer puts his analytical symbols underneath. His *Faust* Symphony also has no Riemannesque numbers underneath, nor do his Debussy analyses.

Let's look at his discussion of Schoenberg's Opus 19, Number 2. He begins to find little configurations and formations that repeat themselves; then he gets to a famous place where there's a very complicated chord (m. 5). Here's the way he analyzes it: he indulges in a very famous hypostatization which is, unfortunately, all too familiar. He says that what you get here is what he's going to call a collection of tones, *Zusatztöne* or *Klirrtöne.*[29] It's untranslatable but means a kind of "fog of tones." The point is that he just gets stuck, absolutely stuck. He then has to invent terms. He's also got material about symmetries. For example, he discusses a very famous return in the Second Quartet of Schoenberg ("F♯-Minor Quartet" it was called). When you get back to the so-called recapitulation (which, in some sense, one can say here), there's a great big fermata. The procedure here became a basis for what was called double leading-tone technique. Everybody was talking about it. What Schoenberg does is converge onto the A, which is the first tone coming back in the upper voice.

EXAMPLE 5-20

In other words, you move into the return not with some dominant seventh chord but with simply a convergence of leading tones from above and below. But what Erpf misses is that while this is true locally, the whole middle section of the piece is on E♭, of which the first chord is enharmonically the true dominant seventh. So, you've got all these duple, multiple functions.

Let us turn to a piece which you may not know. Some of its characteristics will lead us directly into middle Schoenberg. This was once the most played piece in contemporary chamber music. It begins with the unaccompanied first violin, and then the viola enters.

EXAMPLE 5-21

I'm not surprised that none of you recognizes this. I don't think I've heard it live in maybe twenty years, but in the thirties this was one of the standard classics. I'm sure there are some recent recordings. It's the Hindemith Third String Quartet. Hindemith wrote this when he was still considered to be someone who wrote "atonal" music (I'm using their term now, of course). This is an example of technique as it was then practiced. Suppose I said to you, "I have that unaccompanied opening. If I now imitate this canonically (and that's exactly what comes, a canonic imitation of this opening), what note should I enter on?" This becomes a parlor game, yet it's a parlor game that has a certain kind of historical interest, because the answer would have been unambiguous and unequivocal to someone who was living at that time in that idiom. Hindemith would say there is a certain note you *must* answer with, because Hindemith was given to statements like that. What would the note be if you began the answer at the point indicated in the example by an asterisk? The theme was constructed so there'd be an eventual convergence onto what Hindemith would see as a necessary, inevitable note, and that note for Hindemith would have to be an F. Do you see why?

ANSWER: Is it just because there hasn't been an F stated yet?

That's one reason, absolutely. Still, there's one other note that hasn't been stated: B♭. That will be coming along very soon if you start on F, but why not start on B♭? Because if you bring in an F at the asterisk, you get there, as a harmonic interval, a tritone. And the tritone is the only interval you haven't had in the melody. Now that was the way the thinking went, you see. This is certainly contextual (you know how relatively I use that term). It's not because it is a tritone in general. It's simply because a tritone happens to be absent from the melody. It's certainly not that it would always have to be an F but that it's the one that's missing. When that new note enters, it supplies something that hasn't been there before, a new interval and a new pitch. If you had been around Boulanger and the French at all, you would recognize this notion of the "fresh" note. It was a cliché, a Stravinskyan cliché. You saved notes. Look in *Jeu de Cartes* at the way Stravinsky saves an F and brings it in after a rest. That's the fresh note. It was a cliché of the time. There are a lot of funny things in the Stravinsky. But the Hindemith is almost a compendium of techniques of that time; you should look at the third movement, too.

At one time, the most analyzed piece was the *Tristan* Prelude. There's a thesis which simply compares analyses,[30] there's an elaborate Schenkerian analysis of it by Bill Mitchell,[31] Lorenz I've mentioned, and there are others: Ben Boretz's in *Meta-Variations* is an extremely interesting one.[32] Ernst Kurth wrote a whole book about it and about a crisis in music which he saw as generated by it.[33] This book fights about whether some chord was really a dominant or a subdominant, or a double leading-tone chord, or where it would have gone if it had gone where it should have gone—all those things. Kurth also wrote a book on Bach's counterpoint, called *Grundlagen des linearen Kontrapunkts*, in which he analyzed Bach purely linearly.[34] Linear counterpoint became one of the battle cries of a certain music in the late twenties; it is another example of the theorists' "as if." Krenek, Hindemith, Kaminski, and many other composers who regarded themselves as great contrapuntists talked about *lineare Kontrapunkt*. Kurth also wrote a two-volume study of Bruckner and a book on music psychology (not psychology in your sense at all, by the way, but mainly a kind of acoustics). His Ph.D. thesis was a book which would in English be called "The Presuppositions of Harmony" and, like Riemann and Rameau, asked questions like, where does the minor triad come from? (Out of the everywhere!)[35] He did the kinds of things that theorists used to do that really don't interest us very much any more.

But, Kurth was, of all the people around, the one whom one felt most obliged to read. His books were huge and in very difficult German, so one more or less felt that there must be something there. I remember asking Bill Mitchell once if he had read Kurth, because he knew German a great deal better than I did (he had studied with Schenker in Vienna). I asked if he ever found anything in Kurth and he said no. It's one of those great mysteries. I once was stuck on a paragraph of Kurth because the German is absolutely killing (mainly because it doesn't make any sense in any language), and I consulted a member of our German department who was bilingual but didn't know any music. He would translate a sentence and say, "This is the way it goes; does it make any sense?" We weren't being critical about it. He tried to make syntactical sense of it, and I tried to make musical sense of it. We got something out of the paragraph we were working on, but he said, "You know, if I had to translate German like this, I'd charge a hundred dollars a paragraph."

There's nothing in it for me to demean the work of people such as Kurth; it's just very hard to figure out what anybody found in it. Kurth's Bach analyses either were trivial motivic relationships that any child could have found or were utterly and completely vacuous, with such concepts as kinetic energy as opposed to potential energy. Do you know what kinetic energy was? As far as I can ascertain, kinetic energy was when you ascended, and potential energy was when you started high and went low. I'm serious. I never met Kurth, and he has no students or influence in this country. What is interesting, though, is that Schenker did write about Kurth once. In Schenker's analysis of the unaccompanied E-Major Partita of Bach, he said pretty much the same things about him that I'm saying, that it's very difficult to infer what he's talking about or what it has to do with the piece in question.[36]

What these theorists said about *Tristan* reminds me of all the writing on Schoenberg's Opus 16, Number 3; for that, I have my favorite too. It is by a German writer on music, a Berlin journalist who wrote a book on Schoenberg that was considered to be so important that we unenlightened Americans should have a crack at it, and so it was translated into English.[37] In it, this German authority states that in this movement there's an opening chord of five notes, and, after that, nothing changes but the instrumentation. Of course, in all human generosity you can hope only that he's never heard the piece or seen the piece because if anybody ever heard the piece once, he'd know perfectly well the thing that doesn't change after the first measure is the instrumentation and what does change are the pitches. Indeed, it's the *Tristan Prelude* again; it's a canon.

What Schoenberg does is take a symmetrical chord and run with a symmetrical theme.

EXAMPLE 5-22

On the E, he begins a little theme that he then uses explicitly in the middle of the movement. It's very interesting that the fact that this was a strict canon (stricter than the *Tristan* Prelude; this was a strict pitch and temporal canon, the strictest of canons) was totally and completely overlooked for about forty years after the piece was written. And it's through this canonic writing that he arrived at his harmonies—purely contrapuntally (here we go again, associative harmony). These *Five Pieces for Orchestra* are very difficult. They were originally written for a huge orchestra. If you've heard any version of them, you probably haven't heard the original. He wrote a reduced version later on to make it possible for them to be performed by a normal sized orchestra. The publishers said, "Look, you know you really have to put some titles on these movements (like "Madison at Dawn"), so he just made up titles which he hoped would sell his music. The poor man—no matter what he did, he couldn't sell his music. One of the titles actually was the "Changing Chord," so you'd think that this German authority would have at least been aware of this, but it's funny, he wasn't. People heard the chord changing, but they didn't hear how it was changing.

Let me show you some things in the other movements which relate to this. The first movement begins with this little tune.

EXAMPLE 5-23

The first three notes are in the cello alone, and the second three have the cello and oboe together, so, you see, in the instrumentation he tells you how the piece is evolving. He's got a three-note motive which is repeated at a certain transposition, and he will be composing with the tones of the motive. Do you see any relationship between the melody from the first movement (ex. 5-23) and the chord from the third movement (ex. 5-22)?

Once you see it, you'll hear it with the greatest of ease. This is the idea of composing with the tones of a motive: the chord in example 5-22 has a relationship to the motive such that it itself could be regarded as a composing out of that motive. You don't have to know anything more.

The motive in example 5-23 occurs explicitly three times in the first movement. What do you think would be the basis for the transposition of the next statement of the motive? On what transpositional level would he next state these six notes? This is purely associative. This is contextuality carried just about as far as you can imagine. The only presuppositions are the presuppositions of pitch and pitch class and interval. Nothing more. Everything else is being stated within the piece self-sufficiently. Now this is a classical example. One can find much more intricate examples of this kind of thing in *Erwartung* and later in the Opus 22 *Orchestral Songs*. But I think it's much better to stick with the classical examples, the more familiar ones. The next statement of the motive begins on A (m. 36). I'll let you figure out why.

EXAMPLE 5-24

Parenthetically, I must tell you something funny. There is a misprint in some of the editions, wherein the first clarinet has a B in measure 2. Instead, it should be a C. This would give you, embedded in this tiny moment of the piece, the chord from example 5-22. Example 5-25 shows an edition with the misprint, and example 5-26 shows Webern's reduction for two pianos, undertaken under Schoenberg's supervision, with the misprint corrected.

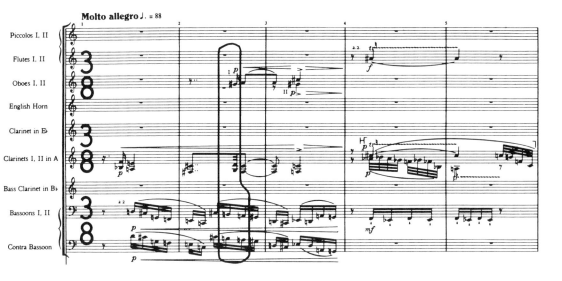

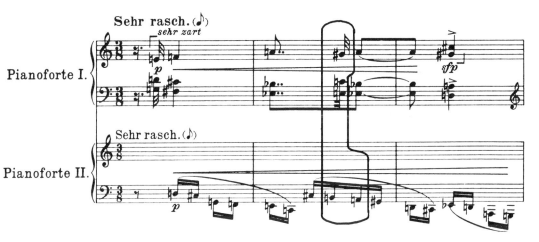

EXAMPLES 5-25 and 5-26

That doesn't explain where the chord comes from; it's just an added plus that he threw in to make your life simpler.

In constructing the chord in example 5-22, all he did was take the first trichord from the first movement and combine it with its own inversion centered around E. The chord was derived from that trichord-type (015), with a note in common where the two trichords overlap (the note in common being that E that's had such a central role) to make it perfectly clear that the chord is symmetrical.

EXAMPLE 5-27

Symmetry is not any kind of geometrical metaphor or anything of this kind. It simply means that you have a chord which is internally redundant, and this involves repetition of intervals.

As the canon progresses, each note of the chord moves in turn. I'm not going to worry about the details of the canon, because it's absolutely mechanical (that's not a critical term). Note by note it moves, and you get these resultant chords.

EXAMPLE 5-28

Then, in measure 227, something very funny happens. In the bass clarinet at the point indicated by an asterisk on the example, F♯ and E suddenly enter. They have nothing to do with the canon, or at least with the explicit function of the canon. The canon hasn't finished yet when he brings in the F♯. Can you figure out now what's going on? If we finished the canon, you would see that you are bound to end up with the same chord a half step lower. Then the harp verifies it in measure 232, and you get the middle part of the movement, which uses this motive specifically in lots of different ways, and then you go back and you repeat the whole thing by inversion. But why F♯–E?

It's so funny the way these things work. It's just like the Hindemith. I have never in my life talked about the Hindemith Third Quartet and this piece together; now it occurs to me that they have certain criteria in common, strangely enough, with regard to these notions of avoidance and saving. What happens is that he states this canon, and then just as he's going to go back to this famous chord and do the whole thing by inversion, you get something which Berg used in *Wozzeck*, a repeated high D—high E (see m. 251). (This may seem like Ars Antiqua to you.) This relates back to the low F♯–E and to the beginning. It indicates that you're getting an inversion around the E. The E is our pivotal tone. In the original five-voice canon, you never had the D, either, so that's the final chromatic completion. He constructed the canon and chord in such a way that, in its original statement, it excludes only D and F♯. You get the F♯–E in the bass clarinet in m. 227; then, toward the end of the movement, you get the D–E, and that signals the inversion returning that finally completes the chromatic of the canon.

When you listen to the first movement, you'll hear these things explicitly. You'll hear an ostinato on D–A–C♯ (see mm. 24ff.), which is, of course, a form of the three-note motive. There are a lot of things which are terribly literal and much more obvious than anything we've talked about here. The second movement, which is based almost entirely upon a single sonority (A–B♭–E♭), has all kinds of continuity techniques of the contextual type. There's a very fancy and very interesting article about it by my colleague Paul Lansky.[38]

The real piece for this sort of thing is the Opus 23, Number 3. It is a complete compendium of everything that was ever done with composing with the tones of a motive; so much so that it turned out to be one of the last pieces in which Schoenberg composed with this technique. That was when he felt that he'd gone just about as far as he could go. There are extraordinary things there that you do not find in these earlier pieces. I wrote about this in an article, "Since Schoenberg."[39] I begin with the various appearances of that five-note motive with which he worked.

EXAMPLE 5-29

Some of it is extremely literal, the modes of continuity are sometimes pretty obvious, until he reaches a great big climax which is based upon a principle that all of you know so very well. He has a five-note motive which at one and only one inversional level is exclusive (that is, in which there is no inter-section of pitch), leaving him two notes to complete the chromatic. Those two notes (C and G) become the basis for the whole end of the piece. So again, we see chromatic completion, collectional implications of an inversion (which means index numbers), associative harmony, and so on.

This is not a piece I advise you to try to play. You can play at it, but it is incredibly hard. In measure 2, he answers the motive with an actual canonic answer.

EXAMPLE 5-30

The crucial place comes much later, where he has the relationship of the motive with a particular position of the inversion, and then he has, believe it or not, augmented triads down below filling in the complete chromatic (it's like the *Faust* Symphony), and these motives also make linear canons and a lot of other things that, when described, sound very perfunctory but they're not. But why did he choose in measure 2 to imitate the motive beginning on F? If anybody says, "Because it's the fifth," I'm leaving, although I think he may have actually done so as a pun.

ANSWER: The F forms the same three-note motive with B–C♯ as the first three notes of the melody.

Exactly. He's getting his harmony purely associatively. You're getting "accustomed to its face." That's exactly the way it works. He's got a five-note motive and he answers beginning on F. With the resulting trichord, he's already articulating a relationship: inversion. His harmony, the basis of his counterpoint, is now derived from the theme itself. And so it goes. This is associative harmony: there's no basis whatsoever for having that trichord have any kind of priority in anybody's music except that he so designated it at the beginning of his piece. If you want contextuality, you can't go much further than that.

6 The Unlikely Survival of Serious Music

Let me begin by apologetically confessing that I do not and I cannot regard the subject of the survival of serious music as one of those subjects so genteel that it can be reserved just for academic or semi-academic occasions by providing a subject so lacking in urgency and pertinence that it can be quietly and safely interred once the occasion has run its course. I must say in this regard that as a composer, but perhaps more pertinently as a teacher of and a colleague of younger composers, that I also don't think that I've stated this subject melodramatically. I don't think there's anything melodramatic or exaggerated about bringing up the question of the actual survival of serious music. I am prepared to admit that I am likely to be more concerned about the survival of my central professional concern, and seem to be more exercised about it, than may seem to many of you to be seemly. But I am not prepared to admit that anything less than, anything other than, sheer survival is at stake, and that such survival seems unlikely when the conditions necessary for that survival are so seriously threatened. These conditions are the corporal survival of the composer in his role as a composer, then the survival of his creations in some kind of a communicable, permanent, and readable form, and finally, perhaps above all, the survival of the university in a role which universities seem less and less able or willing to assume: that is, of the mightiest of fortresses against the overwhelming, outnumbering forces, both within and without the university, of anti-intellectualism, cultural populism, and passing fashion.

Let me assure you, even reassure you, that my subject is not the composer in the university. But it is absolutely impossible to deal with this whole question of music and the composer without dealing with the university centrally. It just so happens that a university setting is where most composers find themselves. So, therefore, the beginnings and ends of this discussion of the state (or, more accurately, the states) of our music will have to do with the fact that we composers are mainly university people. Now, however, the first thing I have to do is disabuse you of any notion that I'm talking about a particular kind of music and a particular kind of university. That would often be inferred, particularly from me, but I mean nothing of the sort. What I'd like to point out rather is that it's become a truism that music—or musical activity, if you wish—has never been so fragmented. Music has never been so pluralistic. This fragmentation, which has induced all kinds of fraternization and all kinds of factionalization, extends just as much to the universities, between universities, among universities, within universities, as anywhere else. And without being aware of this polyglot diversity which is so characteristic of every aspect of our musical activity, we cannot have a substantive discussion of the subject. To confuse these categories and to overlook the fact that we exist in virtually disjunct regions of creative and performance and other activity about music is initially to inhibit and eventually to vitiate any substantive, any realistic, discussion of the field.

So many of the things that I'll have to say may seem to you to be on the one hand overly abstract and on the other hand immensely—perhaps vulgarly—practical. I have to be concerned with both. I know when I discuss this subject, particularly in front of nonprofessionals, I'm accused either of being patronizing or of being paranoid. Now the accusation of patronization usually comes when I say anything about our field whatsoever. I started with the university, for example. Well, the fact that most American composers are university-trained and are university teachers is the most compelling evidence of the intellectual reorientation of music in this country, and not only its intellectual reorientation but also the social reorientation of music in this country. The universities have been obliged to become the havens for—and the patrons of—serious musical activity in all of its manifestations. But this is a condition of which some of our closest academic colleagues are only but barely aware. And they are totally unaware of the profound causes and the profound implications of this condition. So when I talk about this polyglot diversity, this immense diversity of activity—which, admittedly, can lead to antagonisms—we can understand that these antagonisms are usually artificial, because they're founded upon misunderstandings or lack of understanding.

Saying that, I should perhaps indicate something of why this transfer of activity to the universities from the public circuses of music, the citadels of show biz, and the public salons has taken place. It's *not* primarily because of extramusical considerations. One would like to think so—it would ease one's conscience and make one feel that it is a superficial societal condition which will suddenly right itself. But it does not have to do primarily (and certainly not entirely) with the terrifying economics of performance out there in the unreal world or the terrifying growth in the number of scantily educated consumers of historically certified musical products or the ubiquitous controls of journalism. All of these things, of course, have had their effect, but they have not instigated the condition in which we find ourselves, the condition which I'll try to describe and for which I have very little by way of a cure or by way of any kind of optimistic view regarding its eventual outcome.

Rather, we have to start with a realization that music itself has changed. Now here I'm going to sound patronizing to the professionals, and, very soon, I'm going to sound paranoid to the nonprofessionals. Music has changed and it has changed in absolutely fundamental ways which should never be permitted to be minimized by those who would invoke the historical leveling effect of the large historical view. Fifty years ago, when I was a young student of music, we were told, "Look, you're dramatizing yourself. This new music, this music of Schoenberg, Webern, even Stravinsky, is not really that new. It seems new because you're too close to it and because you're part of it, but you're dramatizing yourself and you're making the whole thing a melodramatic situation. You just wait. Either this music will fall into the normal repertoire and will be played as often as the *Surprise* Symphony, or it will simply disappear like an illusion without a future, one of the transitory, evanescent things."

Well, of course, you know, neither has happened. Instead, we've developed different repertoires. The music that is still almost never played by orchestras (I don't want to mention specifics; I don't have to since they're all pretty much the same), and which is not at all in the repertoire of the so-called music lover, not only has become the cornerstone of most young composers' work but also is regarded as a matter of fact, a part of the past. It's already become part of the tradition. The situation of Schoenberg is typical—he was never in fashion and now he's become old-fashioned. This is all part of what has gone on. We've developed these almost disjunct regions of thought and activity. Well, of course, one cannot disregard the consequences of such a situation in thinking about how music has changed, how this fragmentation has taken place which has induced all of this factionalization, in attempting to account for the sources of this factionalization, for this fragmentation, and in attempting to determine why this music is indeed so little listened to and, above all, is likely to be so little performed in the future and is so limitedly performed now.

I'd like to go back and remind you of a very characteristic historical event, an article by Alban Berg, written in 1924, called "What Makes Schoenberg's Music So Difficult to Understand?"[1] Now, I think of that article for a number of reasons. First of all, Berg, who was not an American academician, somehow felt that the understanding of music was reasonable, possible, and even presumably desirable. We won't explicate Berg's notion of understanding, though he attempted to. The idea of understanding music, however, is worth remembering, and it's at least edifying. But what does make Schoenberg's music so difficult to understand? Now when we invoke the notion of difficulty, immediately this notion of paranoia begins to enter. Some say, "Difficult, indeed! Do you revel in your difficulties?" Of course, we don't revel in our difficulties. Believe me, the performance of our difficult music is no revel. I will talk in a moment about what Berg meant about Schoenberg's difficulties, but these difficulties, of course, have accompanying riches and new rewards; otherwise, of course, none of us would be willing to submit ourselves to them. We are not in this sense simply masochistic. But, when Berg began to talk about what makes Schoenberg's music so difficult to understand, it was 1924. Let me place the date for you. In 1924 Schoenberg had written all of that extremely (I will still say) problematical music of the middle period: *Erwartung, Pierrot Lunaire,* the Opus 16 *Orchestra Pieces,* the Opus 22 *Songs,* and so forth. That is not the music that Berg talked about. He could have even talked about the first twelve-tone works, but he didn't talk about those. He chose to talk about Schoenberg's First String Quartet (it's called "in D-Minor"), which couldn't have had any terrors for anyone except that it's rather terrifyingly long.

He chose that work for a very strategic and important reason. If he had talked about *Erwartung* or *Pierrot,* there would have immediately been the notion of the superficial difficulties: those new titillations of the sonic surface; those, perhaps, familiar combinations which didn't go to their familiar destinations at once, or perhaps, ever; that lack of those familiar conjunctions that create patterns, those dimensionally conjoined repetitions which create those patterns which in some places pass for musical form. That is not what he wanted to talk about because, after all, those unfamiliar titillations very soon become standard and very soon become the most familiar of sounds. Those combinations that don't go to their familiar destinations pretty soon find themselves going to destinations on the basis of familiarity and habit. And as for those patterns which create certain kinds of musical forms, listeners very soon found out that it was much more interesting to hear contrapuntalization in such dimensions rather than a conjoining of those dimensions.

So the result was that Berg—whether he was aware of it in precisely the form in which I just formulated it or not—decided to talk about an early piece—a D-minor First String Quartet. Why? Because for him the kind of difficulty that I've been hypothesizing was not a very profound difficulty; it was a passing difficulty, an ephemeral difficulty or set of difficulties. The real difficulty was the extent to which this piece defined its premises within itself, even though it was a D-minor piece, which would seem to suggest right away all the familiarities of the tonal system. In order to hear that piece, in order to follow its sequence of events, in order to follow it as a cumulative containment, a successive subsumption—all those things that musical memory requires if the work eventually is to be entified as a unified totality, an all-of-a-piece of music—you had to listen to that piece very much as a thing in itself. It was defining very many of its own premises within itself, even while the modes of connection, the harmonic aspects of it, the contrapuntal aspects, the rhythmic aspects were still pretty much defined within just a generally shared communal framework of tonality. And this is the crux, of course, of the problem of the diversity. This is when it began. Those middle-period works of Schoenberg, the middle-period works of Berg, the middle-period works of Webern have this particular property in common. They are to as large an extent as possible self-referential, self-contained, and what I'm given to call "contextual." Contextuality merely has to do with the extent to which a piece defines its materials within itself.

Now there are obvious hazards here. The problem of contextuality again is a problem of the listener; it's a problem of the composer; it's a problem of the performer. Just consider what is involved. It means that when you come to hear such a piece, you are listening to a piece which is going to use perhaps physical materials which are familiar, but very little else that is familiar. You're going to have to proceed with this piece by a complete concentration on the piece as piece. You're going to have very little that you can carry with you from your memory of former pieces, very little that you carry by way of your experiences of past music. In other words, it is not very communal—a word to which I will return.

But it had all these new rewards; it had all these new possibilities. The idea of writing a piece which is self-referential, self-contained, is of course an intriguing one, an exciting one, but contextuality is after all a relative thing. Any piece of music is contextual to the extent that when you say, in talking about a piece, that this is related to that, that this is derived from that, that this is a return to that, you're talking contextually. It's a matter of degree, and matters of degree can be crucial where musical intelligibility is concerned. Later, Schoenberg said that the difficulty with this middle period music was indeed the fact that with this contextual approach they could not create structures of great enough length, of great enough complexity.[2] Now immediately that's a very bewildering statement. *Erwartung* isn't long enough? *Erwartung* doesn't have enough notes per square inch? There are very few pieces that have more. He didn't mean that kind of superficial complexity; he didn't mean that kind of superficial temporal length. He meant structural length; he meant structural complexity; he meant degree of structural determination, structural richness. The solution to this problem (which I'm going to say very little about and I don't want you to misinfer my remarks on the basis of my well-known musical associations) for Schoenberg was, of course, the musical formulation of the twelve-tone idea. However, I'm not going to talk much about that. I've talked about that quite enough. But I am going to talk about it as a purely historical or, if you wish, a professional event.

The idea of finding a new communality was absolutely central to Schoenberg's thinking. But when you find a new communality, you have to be sure that the community is going to accept it completely. There has been a complete acceptance of the twelve-tone idea in that composers either accept it, use it, extend it or, more often, react against it or react because of it. But one thing no composer could escape, and that was recognizing that this was an alternative, a viable compositional alternative which seemed to be exciting many composers and which certainly produced works which, whatever one thinks, have been the most pervasively influential works of our time. Again, obviously, this was a revolution in musical thought and any revolution produces its anarchic excesses. But at its core, this was as considered and responsible and thoughtful a revolution as it was pervasive and profound in its influence and in its effects.

Now the reason I've started with this is not because I want to talk about twelve-tone music or because I want to talk about Schoenberg. Rather I want to talk about the beginning of what became this current fragmentation, because this pluralism has created some of our social problems, some of our professional problems, but above all, it has created musical problems. No one denies that it has created problems for the performer, for the listener, and for the composer. Obviously, the performer now picks up a piece and wonders, "Is this a wrong note or not?" He picks up a piece and wonders from the beginning whether his part has been transposed or not. He wonders indeed how to make anything of this piece, and that is the evidence that things have changed rather considerably. We can now pick up a score and wonder whether the score's in C or not. That's not a criticism of music nor of any particular piece. It is simply the most vulgar and direct evidence of the fact that we don't know what assumptions to make about a piece of music when we pick it up. We can do it only by examining the music rather carefully, rather critically, and even then, only sometimes. At this point you could regard all of this as a criticism. But I am not here as a propagandist or an apologist for twelve-tone music or any other kind of music. I'm here to describe a situation; it is probably patronizing to most of you who are musicians—you've lived with it—but to the outside world it still represents a great mystery and a great concern as to why we even do these things. The normal question that would be asked of someone who composes, someone such as I, would be, "Why do you compose under these conditions?" (Sometimes they ask, "Why *don't* you compose?" but that's the other question—the more impertinent one.) The truth is that this is a situation of a complexity that is unequaled in the history of music. We are not dramatizing ourselves. This condition has created our crisis, and the question of how to resolve this crisis involves many other factors.

Now I would talk for a little while about the pure technicalities of this if I felt it would serve any particular purpose. Instead, I will talk only about a few analogies. I don't think it's necessary to go into the technicalities, because I think what is more important is to indicate why I have started talking about the music, why I've started talking about contextuality, why I've talked about the fact that there are subtle relationships between what happened for example in the D-Minor Quartet of Schoenberg and what's happening to most of the music which has been written since, although the D-Minor Quartet hardly seems to be the instigator of a revolution.

But when I talk about Schoenberg's early music and what it instigated, I could also talk, for example, about what Schoenberg's thought about music and thought in music did to our whole thinking about the music of the past. The music of Schoenberg (and, of course, in this particular case I take him to be the central figure) has made us think just as differently about the music of the past as Schenker's theory of the music of the past has made us think differently about the music of the present, perhaps even of the future. But Schoenberg and Schenker, whom I shall be speaking of more in a moment, shared one remarkable characteristic that they would never have admitted. They both were very much concerned to engage in minimum mutilation of the past. Schoenberg thought of himself, of course, as a member of that great German tradition: Bach, Mozart, Beethoven, Brahms. He was part of that and he had to define his relationship to it, just as Schenker, for example, felt that his theory grew out of Carl Philipp Emanuel Bach, out of eighteenth-century theorists. He was no revolutionary. They were both, to coin a cliché, reluctant revolutionaries, or revolutionaries in spite of themselves.

But this revolution in Schoenberg's thought is so subtle in many respects that, for example, one finds it very difficult to explain why the usual criticism of twelve-tone music—and I hesitate to bring this up, but I have to—is so utterly silly. In fact, I'm going to supply you with a better criticism of it. It used to be said frequently, for example, that the trouble with the whole twelve-tone idea is that it's too mechanical, too mechanistic, and it forces too many things upon you. You don't have the great freedom of will which artists of the past enjoyed. The truth is that if anyone is concerned to dismiss a whole body of music—and it's a rather futile and undesirable pastime—I would suggest you could say quite the opposite. You could say the trouble with any twelve-tone work, by virtue of the whole notion of the twelve-tone concept, is that it's too contextual. It's too self-contained. The communal aspect shared by a twelve-tone work, and therefore what you can bring from one twelve-tone work to another or even from one piece of the same composer to another, is really not enough. It's not enough to make that piece communal enough so that you won't have many of the same dangers of the more highly contextual music of the middle period.

Let me show you for just a second what that means, although this will be old stuff to some of you and perhaps unintelligible to others—this is the danger that one always runs. The constraints of twelve-tone writing (to the extent that a piece can be called twelve-tone at all) are nothing more than a principle of formation of the most characteristic, the most familiar physical materials—the twelve pitch classes of the usual chromatic scale—and certain principles of transformation which are interval preserving. Now the notion of interval, of course, is the fundamental scaling principle of all the music of the past. One has to assume intervallic scaling and intervallic perception or you don't have any of the music that you certainly regard as the music that we have. In addition you have the twelve chromatic pitch classes. That's nothing new. They've been used for a long, long time since well-tempered claviers and so forth were talked about. So the material is not new. The primitives of the perception are not new. What is new?

Well, what is new is so subtle that it can be described only by analogy. When you go into an elementary harmony course and someone plays an interval and says, "This interval usually proceeds so," they're saying something which is generally true in a great deal of tonal music. They are indicating a contingency, a dependency which is true of a great deal of tonal music by virtue of triadic considerations, scale considerations, and so on. What remains, for example, in a tonal piece to make it tonal—not a sufficient condition but a necessary condition—is certainly the fact that certain pitch contingencies change, but intervallic contingencies don't change throughout the piece. This is, of course, an important, a primary aspect of any piece of music: what's going to change in the course of the piece and what's going to remain a fixity, a constancy.

Now you suddenly see a very subtle analogy between the twelve-tone and the tonal ideas. In a twelve-tone piece, by virtue of the whole notion of an ordering of the twelve pitch classes, the interval structure is indeed going to remain the same—the contingencies, the dependencies are going to remain the same throughout the piece—while the pitch contingencies change, just as in a tonal piece. I am referring to what happens in a tonal piece when you tonicize or modulate or whatever word you care to use. The difference, however, is that the intervallic contingencies of tonal music remain fixed for all tonal pieces. The intervallic contingencies for a twelve-tone piece are defined internally by the structure of the set, which is defined within the piece. That is it. No more than that need you know. The result is that the simplest operation that you ever encounter in tonal music, such as transposition, in-duces in twelve-tone music a totally different set of hierarchical criteria.

When Schoenberg was talking about his middle period in music he called it "composing with the tones of a motive." Well, what's a motive? A motive is something defined within the piece. Now, the twelve-tone set is not a motive, though some mistakenly conceive of it as a motive or a theme. But the idea of composing with the tones of a motive—the ultimate contextual idea with regard to musical structure—certainly is an enormous and giant step when elaborated into the twelve-tone idea. The truth of the matter is, however, that some of the old problems still remain. And many of those problems are still problems for the listener, problems for the performer.

Imagine you're listening to a tape of a language that you have never heard in your life and of which you know nothing. It has no relation to any language that you know at all, so you cannot possibly extrapolate in any way whatsoever from any of your past language knowledge or habits. You're asked just to define the segmentations of this language, to discover when words end, or what are the phonemes of the language, or any of the primitive building blocks of the language. Just imagine the problem involved and imagine either the kind of approaches you might take to hearing it, or the approaches a person might take in order to finally get some notion of the purely syntactical nature (not, of course, the semantic nature) of this particular language. That is the contextual situation. Now I've concentrated on what I have to regard as the musical core of our crisis. This is it. It has splintered our musical society; it has in many ways isolated musical society from the rest of society within the academy.

There are two other aspects of this crisis which I have to mention. One of them has to do with what probably most people regard as the revolutionary aspect of our field at this time, and that's the electronic. Well, of course, it smacks of revolution. It carries with it the implications of the confrontation of man by a machine: the displacement of the performer—a new economic crisis. Well, it's all of those things in a very mild and trivial way. Much more profoundly, it is not the instigator of any musical revolution whatsoever. It is the child of a revolution, perhaps. But the electronic technology was available long before any serious composer felt impelled to use it, because he didn't have the musical impulse that required him to turn to the medium.

To speak of electronic music is, of course, not to speak of a music in any sense of an idiom or a style or a compositional disposition or compositional techniques. Obviously this most vast and flexible of media imposes least by way of style or idiom (whatever those ill-defined terms may mean to you) upon the composer. On the contrary, the whole point here is that we have a whole new set of boundary conditions, and those boundary conditions are worth noting. When I refer to the electronic medium, I don't mean a performance medium, and I don't mean the keyboard. I mean the purely electronic medium, be it as it mainly is today, the computer, or as it was for me, the RCA synthesizer, the programmable synthesizer which I'm not going to speak of anymore, I promise you. This medium puts the composer in a totally different relationship to the materials of music. He must make every single decision for himself, and the main decision that he has to make for himself (beyond the compositional decisions, which, of course, are going to be interrelated) is what the human being can hear.

I suppose I'm leading into something which I somehow inevitably find myself wishing to confront, and that is the old accusation that the human element is lacking in electronic music. If that is said just polemically I won't countenance it. But if it's said in genuine misunderstanding, there's a very simple answer. Electronic music is created by—I hope—a human composer who has to inform this dumb machine of every aspect of his musical decisions. And then the receptor is the human being, and now the only boundary conditions are those very mysterious, intricate conditions of the perceptual and conceptual capacities of the human auditor. The intervention of the acoustical piano is much more of a mechanical intervention. It imposes much more by way of a limitation between the composer and the receptor than any electronic instrument. But, indeed, what we do have to know more of is what the human being can hear, what he can remember, what he can contain, what he can process, if you wish to use that word. And when we ask these questions—and we've had to ask them in order to be able to use these instruments to the full extent of their capacities—we've learned a great deal about how we hear all music, not only electronic but nonelectronic music as well. At the moment what we know is just how little we know about such matters. But the misunderstanding about composers turning to the electronic domain is germane to what I was saying first.

There were any number of people who seemed to have the notion that composers turned to electronics because they wanted new sounds. They were supposed to have been dissatisfied with the sound of the symphony orchestra. Nothing could be farther from the truth. First of all, composers were not dissatisfied with sheer sound. They were dissatisfied with a lot of other things, but not with the sound of conventional or acoustical instruments. There was no such dissatisfaction. Furthermore, a composer knows better than anyone else that a new timbre becomes old quicker than anything in the world. What composers were dissatisfied with was the situation of the temporal aspect of music. Whether with T. S. Eliot you say music moves only in time or, a little more chicly, you say that any piece of music can be described by a time series, the temporal aspect of music is of course a central aspect, a central dimension. One has to think about time whenever one is thinking of music.

But time in the sense of rhythm is not that glibly disposed of. We know perfectly well that there are musical instruments which provide automatic or semiautomatic means of producing a pitch, but not of producing a duration. Any performer knows that the mental imagery involved in reproducing a pitch, no matter what the instrument, is very different from the mental imagery of reproducing a duration or an attack point. That is what led most of the composers to the electronic domain originally. It was not only because of the rhythmic problems of individual performance, or the ensemble performance of rhythm, but because of the whole rhythmic question—rhythm in every sense of the aspect. It was not only the individual linear rhythm or the compounding of those linear rhythms into ensemble rhythms, but the rhythm of timbre, the rhythm of register, the time rate of change of the volume of sound—all of these things, most of which could not be controlled, but all of which are audible. The primary thing about the electronic domain is that anything that you can hear you can structure, and, of course, that is simply not true of any other domain. And in wishing to structure time in all of its manifestations, much of the impetus came from the concern with serialism, twelve-tone serialism. Because once one thinks of that referential norm of a piece of music as being an ordering in time, then, of course, what does one think about? One thinks about the electronic domain and how to achieve that ordering to the full degree of one's capacity to discriminate aurally.

There's another aspect, other than the electronic, which is part of this revolution, but which doesn't seem as revolutionary at all, and which seems always to be, of course, highly academic. I'll say a few words about that, and that is words about music. Back in the early fifties when we saw that we were in trouble, when we saw that we didn't have the appropriate audience (and we do concern ourselves about such things, if only for selfish reasons), we thought that perhaps we could appeal to our fellow intellectuals by impressing them with the seriousness of our words. We thought we would attract them with our words about music and this would eventually lead them to the sound of our music. Well of course our words went as unheeded as our music went unheard. But we learned a lesson. We discovered that what induces even more resentment than taking music seriously is taking talking about music seriously. This is not a trivial concern. You know, in the beginning is the work, and these days in the beginning with the work is the word about the work. Music is talked about before it is listened to, while it's listened to, and instead of being listened to.

And who does this talking about the music which determines what is the little bit that's recorded, the tiny bit that is published, and, therefore, what can be heard, and therefore what is listened to, and therefore what is learned, and eventually, therefore, what is composed? Well this talking is done mainly by a group of past and present masters of the detached normative, the dangling evaluative, those who have created an epistemological situation which is usually satisfied by a self-comforting tautology: "If I don't understand it, it's not worth understanding; therefore I understand everything worth understanding." We in music seem to be the only ones who are living in that impossible world in which unjustified false belief not only parades as but is published as knowledge. We have a very serious situation in that regard. Music has become the final resting place for all of those hoary psychophysical dualisms such as heart and brain, the cognitive and the sentient. Well, we're having a problem and that is part of our problem. The notion of serious discourse about music is a concern to me not because I have to be concerned essentially about the state and fate of discourse, but because I'm concerned about the state and fate of music.

Now, of course, it's true of any revolutionary period that it examines and rescrutinizes its own past. And in music this took the form of rescrutinizing the scrutinies of the music of the past—by which I mean examining what passed for theory in the past. Now here I mention Heinrich Schenker again. It certainly was not in this letter but it was in this spirit that he began to formulate his analytical theory of music. Again, I won't offer any great discourse here on technicalities of Schenker, but rather just the fact that this man, who was the most archreactionary with regard to his musical tastes and disposition, was Schoenberg's equal as a revolutionary. He too was a Viennese. He and Schoenberg were not very good friends and both of them were totally unaware of the Viennese circle. All of them were living right around the Ringstrasse and they probably could have helped each other a great deal, but I assure you they didn't. Still, it's amazing to see what Schenker did without any methodological preparation, without any formal concerns. What he did was create a theory. It is a theory; it can be formalized. It is a theory even by reasonable standards, so it's certainly a theory by any musical standard. He suddenly discovered that all the regularities that meant a great deal to him in the music of the past, and seemed to mean a great deal to other composers and other observers of music, could not be entailed within the theory of the past. If they were adjoined to that theory, they had to be adjoined as new, independent, unrelated assumptions.

Schenker's theory has two remarkable aspects: its explanatory scope and the fact that his analyses can be tested by synthesis. Schenker indeed is at the moment one of the most remarkable phenomena on our scene—both our academic scene and our musical scene. Back in the 1930s the name of Schenker was an underground name. I've told so many anecdotes about Schenker and his relation to life in this country at that time that I'm going to spare you them. However, I will tell you that there was no one in any university who was teaching Schenker analysis at that time except one man who sneaked in a little bit in a freshman course at Columbia, and if the chairman of his department had caught him teaching Schenker, he'd have been summarily fired.[3] Well, the point is that Schenker was indeed a heretic. And now as I have already said, Schenkerism has become hieratic. It has transformed its function completely. That has not happened to Schoenberg in quite the same way. Schenker theory has insinuated itself—and I use that word only as a descriptive—into virtually elementary textbooks. He's still basically misunderstood, but it does indicate how desperately we need the academic, because it's happened in the academic. It hasn't affected anything out there. It hasn't affected in the slightest those who determine the fates of, at least, performers and conductors and others. It affects our fates indirectly. But you see, what I'm trying to say is that as music grows out, it grows up, and it needs so many of the resources of the university. Schenker couldn't have happened without the university in the same way I don't think Schoenberg could have. Electronics could not have. Computer analysis could not have. Computer production of sound could not have. So you see I'm now back to the university.

Perhaps you assume I'm describing an idyllic condition for the composer. Now comes the paranoia. The idyllic condition is much more by way of an uneasy alliance. Now to be sure many composers enter the university and forego their relations to the great world out there. But they relinquish only with reluctance those very fragile ties to the great world of public music. Somehow they think they can eat their crumbs and have them too. Well, that hasn't worked very well, because, for such composers in the university, it means they're always regarded as in some sense traitors to their intellectual class. For composers the response to such a charge is very simple. It's that they've never been really admitted to this class. They are not provided the kind of academic positions that are awarded to those in other fields. Their professional needs are not satisfied in anything like the same way. Their music is not published as it should be by university presses. Their music is not recorded. They cannot communicate with their colleagues in the same way that most members of other fields can.

These are not to be regarded as complaints at the moment. I simply want to define a kind of condition that exists. The situation with regard to colleagues in the university varies obviously from university to university. I remember when I was out at Bowling Green for a festival, we were having a discussion for all university composers, as most of us are, of course. I pointed out the fact that at my university, Princeton, when we gave the best conceivable concert of contemporary music—and that meant the Schoenberg Serenade and other classics of the twentieth century—by absolutely the best performers you could possibly get from New York, a concert which included the best performance of the Schoenberg Serenade I had ever heard, we had a small audience of perhaps seventy-five or one hundred people. No one from any other department of the university was present. A young man from Bowdoin College said he thought that this would not be true at other, smaller schools, where the members of the faculty do not regard themselves as having their own important work to do and are not just going to regard music as providing some sort of surcease from it. I think he has a point. But although I'm often alleged to have a scientific bias (something I admit only to the extent that I admit that a few of my best friends are scientists), what the scientists have provided me with are some remarkable materials supporting my feelings about the way the composer is viewed in at least some academia.

I am from a university and I'm speaking mainly of the university. But I also teach in a conservatory, Juilliard, and, if in the university I'm obliged to justify the position of music, in the conservatory I'm obliged to justify the position of the living composer; so either way you have a battle. In the university, the composer is usually regarded by his colleagues in other fields as a failed composer. I mean if he were a real composer, he'd be out in the fields of radio and radar and Hollywood, Broadway, and really making it. They think first that music, after all, is show biz. Secondly, there's always the very strong suspicion that these lectures that we offer in our classrooms are just less successful versions of those disquisitions on music which are available on television. After all, aren't those the honeyed words of a Harvard man?

I have something that I would like to read to you to support this. I've used it before because I haven't found anything quite as delectable. A number of years ago, 1966 as a matter of fact, there was a panel at Columbia University on the secrets of life. Now I don't want you to think that this title in any sense is to be taken as one of these light journalistic affairs. It wasn't. It was a very heavy conference indeed, and it involved a biologist and a mathematician and a philosopher and a physicist, all very eminent men. Therefore, I'm not going to tell you their names as I read this quotation about their verbal activity at this particular moment, because I'd like to conceal the identity of the guilty. This is a newspaper report. Now since the newspaper in question is one that is notably untrustworthy, I went and listened to this tape, and I can vouch for the fact that, except for some rather vulgar descriptive language, this is accurate. Let me quote the newspaper. "The biologist's pique turned to pleasure as the panel gamboled for nearly fifteen minutes with the musical analogy. The chairman inspired this excursion when he read a quotation. It proposed that to seek physical and chemical explanations of life as a final goal of biology was like hoping that a logical analysis could provide the explanation of a Bartok quintet. The physicist said that he was not so sure of the absurdity of that proposition. 'Not at all,' he said, 'because we've all heard of the new music being composed right out of the analysis and being built up in this way.' 'Oh boy!' the mathematician broke in. 'Have you heard it?' "[4]

Now although this playlet continued, I trust that this is enough to give you a flavor of the situation. First of all, what I particularly liked at this time, 1966, was that they went on and on; fifteen minutes, remember, this all lasted, and I listened to every, every word of it. I noticed that most of you were so well-mannered that you didn't laugh out loud at that knowing reference to a Bartok quintet. Well in 1966, if you looked in the right places, you could have discovered that indeed there had been two Bartok quintets. They were both juvenilia and neither had been published. One was unfinished and no musician I know had known any Bartok quintet, but these scientists seemed to know them intimately. I'm not just baiting scientists; I'm going to be baiting other people, too, in a moment. The fact is that as a result of this, the Juilliard Quartet went out and found this early Bartok quintet, got it from Bartok's son, and they've since played it. They too, of course, had read this newspaper account about a Bartok quintet.

Now beyond that there are much more serious implications of this. For example, I don't quite know what music the physicist was referring to when he talked about "the new music being composed right out of the analysis and being built up in this way." I have no idea of what procedures he thought he was misdescribing or what music he thought he was characterizing. I would like to know at least one specific work, because obviously, if you believe the mathematician, if you had heard one, you wouldn't have heard them all. I'm also amazed that scientists could so misuse the notion of logical analysis—what is a logical analysis of a Bartok quintet or even a quartet? This verbiage! This absolute irresponsibility! I'd like to think of what would happen if I as a musician were under the same circumstances, at a serious panel, and said, "Boy! Have you seen this stuff they call modern mathematics? You know it has no numbers or anything, just words like homotopy and omalogy—oh boy!"

Since most of the people on that panel could obviously state the second law of thermodynamics with a great deal of elegance and eloquence, you may think that this is a skirmish and a renewed battle of the two cultures. Far be it from me to start that again, because I found myself too often stationed in that one-man's land directly in the line of both fires. (As a matter of fact, my only disagreement with the notion of the two cultures is the conservatism of its cardinality.) It takes me back to the very beginning of where I began to talk today. But I have, in another place at another time (and I shan't read it to you now), documented the cavalier presumptions of a whole host of non-scientists and scientists with regard to music because it is symptomatic of this whole condition, this kind of presumption. In that particular array it began with an intellectual historian (or anti-intellectual historian), then a mighty computer mite, then a master of that reification called aesthetics, and finally a self-defined, self-made, self-righteous polymath, or renaissance man. Anyone who's interested in seeing these quotations can find them in an article of mine.[5] But I do have a couple that I thought you should cherish because one of these I buried in a footnote and the other I've never published.

There's a celebrated sociologist who wrote an article which I would never refer to, except it's had such circulation. First it was published in *Daedalus* and then it was published in a book called *Science and*—if you'll forgive the expression—*Culture*, and it has been literally quoted to me or quoted to me literally dozens of times. Now the sociologist's name I shall again conceal, but you would all know the name. I'm also going to quote something from a colleague of his in a moment, so then perhaps you'll be able to identify him. Here's what he says: "Modern music, taking Schoenberg as its turning point, becomes obsessed with sound alone."[6]

Of all contemporary music and of all contemporary composers he chose Schoenberg, the arch-pitch-composer! I tell you what I suggest. I propose that we offer a little prize as a very simple rejoinder to that particular statement.

What we'll do is offer a prize to complete the following sentence: "Modern sociology, taking Max Weber as its turning point, becomes obsessed with ————." Complete in one word or less.

I'm sure that some of you will say that no one takes sociologists seriously anyway, but there are a number of my colleagues who do indeed seem to feel that linguists can be very important guides to their work, and who regard them in some cases as intellectual flugelmen. So now I have a quotation from the very celebrated linguist who teaches at the same institution as did the sociologist whom I just quoted. I won't identify the institution except to say that it's noted for its large collection of certified public professors and its high salaries. The quotation is from a book called *Aspects of Language.* Please listen to this: "In music the fundamental gives the message, the overtones the movement."[7] You're not going to laugh? Well, I guess if you didn't laugh, it is because there must be a lot of you people trying to write music with sinusoidal oscillators. But so be it.

I warned you of the paranoia, but we do have problems as composers. I can document this personally. I can certainly document this professionally. It's not a matter of personal pique. It's a matter of what's happening to our products, what's happening to our communications, what's happening to our profession. Sometimes we are particularly saddened by the fact that even within our little humble house, people who should be on our side of the two-culture alley and living in the same abode take this position with regard to composers. I mean there are those (and again this is not to be construed as a universal or as any kind of baiting) who feel that composers really shouldn't be in the university. This concern often takes the fraternal form that could be described as, "What's a nice composer like you doing in a place like this? You should be out free and unfettered and, incidentally, unfed." They feel that theirs is the noble task of educating the educable; ours is that of titillating the illiterate. The motives here may be as obvious as they are odious, but we do have to live with this.

To consign us to the great world out there, however seriously or however viciously, is to consign us to oblivion. Out there in that world outside the university, our music and our words are bound to fall on unheeding or, at least, uncomprehending ears. Don't forget, out there we're an academic, and there's no more sturdy vestige of anti-intellectualism than the fact that the very term *academic* is conceived to be an immediate, automatic, and ultimate term of derogation. Whereas in any other field of creative intellection it is assumed that the most informedly problematical, the most responsibly advanced work will usually take place in the academy, somehow this is not so with regard to the composer. The other thing that you must realize is that out there we're Americans. We're American composers. Now if the best thing a composer can be is dead, the next best thing he can be is German. The worst thing, one of the worst things he can possibly be, still, is American.

You're going to say paranoia again. I think I'd like to document this in two ways, one that will be particularly relevant to those of you here and another that is actually a little more profoundly indicative of the situation. When my daughter was a college student, she brought home one day a magazine which I am told was the most preferred among college students. I won't tell you the name of the magazine, but from that description you can infer that it isn't the *Journal of Symbolic Logic* or *Perspectives of New Music*. This magazine gave a culture quiz to a number of young women from any number of our best institutions. I'm not being sardonic; they are probably our best institutions. I don't know whether the University of Wisconsin was included— I just simply don't remember. These women were asked their favorite novelists. And boy, did they conform. Their favorite novelists were Joyce and Proust and Faulkner. Then they were asked their favorite composers. I have to read this; otherwise I can't remember these names: first, Bob Dylan, then John Lennon, then Henry Mancini.

I'm not concerned about their tastes. That is not what interests me in the slightest. If I had been asked that when I was fifteen, I may have said DeSylva, Brown, and Henderson. That is not what concerns me; rather, it's the different cultural attitude. It's the different connotation of simply the word *composer*. They didn't mean *songwriter;* they meant *composer*. This is a confusion. They didn't name, for any of their favorite novelists, any mystery writers. They didn't say Agatha Christie or Dashiell Hammett or one of their romance writers. But those would have been applicable or comparable in any reasonable sense.

I have a much more interesting example—at least interesting for me. This is mainly directed to the composers here. In 1957 a well-known German philosopher and academic then at the University of Cologne named Ludwig Landgrebe wrote a book the title of which was *Philosophie der Gegenwart,* or "Contemporary Philosophy."[8] This was a book covering contemporary philosophy. It had a bibliography of over two hundred items which the book referred you to and on which the book drew. There was only one book in the English language listed in that bibliography, a book by a man named Stace, a very little remembered Anglo-American philosopher who fortunately or unfortunately happened to have been at Princeton or I wouldn't have known the name.[9] Quite characteristically, his name was misspelled in the bibliography as Stage rather than Stace. There was no mention of any English philosopher. Imagine a book on philosophy with no Bertrand Russell, no John Austin, of course no Americans, no Quine, no Goodman, no one of that kind. And above all, no Germans or Austrians who had left Germany or Austria. In other words there was no Carnap, there was no Popper, there was no Bergmann, not even a Wittgenstein, and after all he was a pretty popular figure by this time.

But what I'm telling you this for is that when this book was translated into English and published in New York, the publisher felt for both moral and professional reasons he had to change the name of that volume. It became *Major Problems in Contemporary European Philosophy*, and that bibliography in the back was changed to "Selected Bibliography—most important writings of European philosophers." That's what it became in English. In 1958, just a year later, the publication *Die Reihe* was published in Austria. It had an issue called *Young Composers*. Young Composers, indeed! They were only European composers. No British composers, of course no American composers, no other composers, but it was called *Young Composers*. A year later that was translated into English and it was published by Theodore Presser, which after all publishes a lot of American composers. Do you know what they changed the name of that volume to? *Young Composers*.[10] That shows you the moral and commercial pressures which make our life very different.

I may seem to be extremely negative at this point. Particularly since I'm facing the end of all of this, I do want to tell you that we have a few people who are voices in the wilderness on our side who don't happen to be musicians. There's a quotation, which I'm almost going to end with, from Nelson Goodman. This is the kind of quotation that you're not likely to encounter very often from almost anybody in any field, and since this was buried away in a small magazine article, I'd like to read it to you. He says, "My argument that the arts must be taken no less seriously than the sciences is not that the arts "enrich" or contribute something warmer or more human, but that the sciences, as distinguished from technology, and the arts, as distinguished from fun, have as their common function the advancement of understanding."[11] Now that coming from a musician would seem absolutely unwarrantedly pretentious. I can assure you that the understanding of which he was talking here was not that kind of understanding which reduces the rich manifestations, the rich ramifications, of musical relationships to some mundane banalities, not some sort of many-one mapping of all those wonderfully rich ramifications of musical relations to some sort of representation of the world out there. What he meant was understanding, understanding of music and understanding of a great many other things by a fairly obvious process.

I'm not going to try to summarize, and I've certainly not offered you anything more than what is a description of one aspect of this crisis in music, with no solution being offered because I know of no solutions. I think therefore you can understand why those of us who dare to presume to attempt to make music as much as it can be rather than as little as one can get away with—music's being under the current egalitarian dispensation—and who've entered the university as our last hope, our only hope, and ergo our best hope, hope only that we're not about to be abandoned.

Notes / Glossary / Index

Notes

1. The Twelve-Tone Tradition

1 Lehman Engel (b. Jackson, Mississippi, 1910; d. 1982) studied at the Cincinnati College of Music and with Rubin Goldmark at Juilliard; he also had private lessons with Roger Sessions. Engel was a composer of choral and theater music.

2 *The Musical Leader: A Weekly Record of Musical Events, Dramatic and Society Topics.*

3 Letter from Schoenberg to Fritz Reiner, 29 October 1944. *Arnold Schoenberg Letters*, ed. Erwin Stein, trans. E. Wilkins and E. Kaiser (London: Faber and Faber, 1958), 222.

4 Marion Bauer, *Twentieth-Century Music: How It Developed and How to Listen to It* (New York: G. P. Putnam's Sons, 1933). Reprinted with a new Introduction by Milton Babbitt (New York: Da Capo Press, 1978).

5 Arnold Schoenberg, "Composition with Twelve Tones," in *Style and Idea*, ed. Leonard Stein, trans. Leo Black (Berkeley: University of California Press, 1984), 223.

6 This expression appears in Document 173 of the Schoenberg Archive. Reported by Jan Maegaard in "A Study in the Chronology of Op. 23–26 by Arnold Schoenberg," *Dansk Aarbog for Musikforskning* 2 (1962): 93.

7 Norbert Von Hannenheim (b. 1898; d. ?) studied with Schoenberg in Berlin from 1929 to 1931.

8 Adolph Weiss (b. 1891; d. 1971) was a composer and bassoonist and was the first American to study with Schoenberg in Berlin (1925–26). "The Lyceum of Schönberg," *Modern Music* 9 (1932): 99–107.

9 For a discussion of combinatoriality, see Milton Babbitt, "Some Aspects of Twelve-Tone Composition," *The Score and I.M.A. Magazine* 12 (1955): 53–61.

10 Arnold Schoenberg, *Structural Functions of Harmony*, ed. Leonard Stein, rev. ed. (New York: Norton, 1969).

11 Patricia Carpenter.

12 Personal communication from Igor Stravinsky to Milton Babbitt.

13 Paul Nordoff (b. 1909; d. 1977) was head of composition at Philadelphia Conservatory (1938–43) and later taught at Michigan State College (1945–49) and Bard College (1948–59).

14 Leonard Stein.

2. Contextual Counterpoint

1 John Perkins, "Dallapiccola's Art of Canon," *Perspectives of New Music* 1/2 (1963): 95–106.

2 Milton Babbitt, "Since Schoenberg," *Perspectives in New Music* 12/1-2 (1973–74): 3–28.

3. Large-Scale Harmonic Organization

1 Igor Stravinsky and Robert Craft, *Memories and Commentaries* (Berkeley: University of California Press, 1981), 91.

4. Questions of Partitioning

1 Examples 4-1 through 4-5 and 4-14 through 4-17 and some of the accompanying theoretical material may also be found in Milton Babbitt, "Since Schoenberg," *Perspectives of New Music* 12/1 (1974): 3–28.

2 David Lewin, "The Intervallic Content of a Collection of Notes, Intervallic Relations between a Collection of Notes and Its Complement: An Application to Schoenberg's Hexachordal Pieces," *Journal of Music Theory* 4/1 (1960): 98–101.

3 Milton Babbitt, "Stravinsky's Verticals and (Schoenberg's) Diagonals: A Twist of Fate," in *Stravinsky Retrospectives*, ed. Ethan Haimo and Paul Johnson (Lincoln, Neb.: University of Nebraska Press, forthcoming).

4 Eric Walter White, *Stravinsky: The Composer and His Works* (London: Faber and Faber, 1979), 506.

5 Jerome Kohl, "Exposition in Stravinsky's Orchestral *Variations*," *Perspectives of New Music* 18 (1979–80): 391–406.

5. Professional Theorists and Their Influence

1 Milton Babbitt, "The Music Theoretician's Dilemmas," keynote address at the Annual Conference of the Society for Music Theory, Los Angeles, California, 1981.

2 *High Fidelity Magazine* 31/4 (April 1981): 62.

3 Simon Sechter, *Die Grundsätze der musikalischen Komposition*, 3 vols. (Leipzig: Breitkopf and Härtel, 1853–54). First volume edited and translated by Carl

Christian Muller as *The Correct Order of Fundamental Harmonies* (New York: W. A. Pond, 1871; 12th ed., 1912).

4 William Mitchell, *Elementary Harmony* (Englewood Cliffs, N.J.: Prentice-Hall, 1939).

5 Felix Salzer and Carl Schachter, *Counterpoint in Composition: The Study of Voice Leading* (New York: McGraw-Hill, 1969).

6 Letter from C. P. E. Bach cited by Kirnberger in his *Die Kunst des reinen Satzes in der Musik* (Berlin: H. S. Rottmann, 1771–79), vol. 2, pt. 3, p. 188.

7 Walter Piston, *Harmony* (New York: Norton, 1941; 3d ed., 1962).

8 Salzer and Schachter, *Counterpoint in Composition*, 264–65.

9 Ibid., 265.

10 Wiesbaden: Breitkopf and Härtel, 1927 (reprinted in 1969).

11 Maury Yeston, ed., *Readings in Schenker Analysis and Other Approaches* (New Haven: Yale University Press, 1977).

12 David Beach, "Beethoven, *Piano Sonata Op. 53*, Introduzione: A Schenkerian Analysis," ibid., 204–16.

13 Ernst Oster, "Re: A New Concept of Tonality(?)," *Journal of Music Theory* 4 (1960).

14 Salzer's analysis appears in his *Structural Hearing: Tonal Coherence in Music* (New York: Dover Publications, 1962), vol. 2, ex. 430.

15 Hermann Erpf, *Studien zur Harmonie und Klangtechnik der neueren Musik* (1927; reprint, Wiesbaden: Breitkopf and Härtel, 1969), 128.

16 Arnold Schoenberg, *Structural Functions of Harmony*, ed. Leonard Stein, rev. ed. (New York: Norton, 1969).

17 Heinrich Schenker, *Five Graphic Analyses* (New York: Dover Publications, 1969).

18 Oswald Jonas, "Mozarts ewigen Melodie," *Der Dreiklang: Monatsschrift für Musik* (April 1937–February 1938): 86–87.

19 Charles Burkhart, "Schenker's 'Motivic Parallelisms,' " *Journal of Music Theory* 22 (1978): 145–66.

20 See, for example, Christopher Simpson, *The Division-Violist, or, An Introduction to the Playing upon a Ground* (London, 1659).

21 Henry Purcell, "A Brief Introduction to the Art of Descant: or, Composing Musick in Parts," in J. Playford, *An Introduction to the Skill of Musick*, 12th ed. (London, 1694; reprint, New York: Da Capo Press, 1972).

22 E. Hertzmann, C. Oldman, D. Heartz, and A. Mann, eds., *Thomas Attwoods Theorie- und Kompositionsstudien bei Mozart* in *Mozart: Neue Ausgabe sämtlicher Werke*, Supplement, Werkgruppe 30, Band 1 (Kassel: Bärenreiter, 1965).

23 Johann Mattheson, *Der Volkommene Capellmeister* (Hamburg: C. Herold, 1739).

24 Peter Westergaard, *An Introduction to Tonal Theory* (New York: Norton, 1975).

25 J. Stettenheim, *Tribune*, Berlin, 6 February 1873.

26 Salomon Jadassohn, *Melodik und Harmonik bei Richard Wagner*, 1899.

27 Alfred Lorenz, *Das Geheimnis der Form bei Richard Wagner*, 4 vols. (Berlin: M. Hesse, 1924–33; facsimile ed. Tutzing: Hans Schneider, 1966).

28 Antoine Reicha, *Art du compositeur dramatique: Un cours complet de composition vocale* (Paris: S. Richault, 1833).

29 Hermann Erpf, *Studien*, 188.

30 Edward Duffy, "Four Analyses of the Prelude to Tristan: A Review" (undergraduate thesis, Princeton University, 1975).

31 William Mitchell, "The Tristan Prelude: Techniques and Structure," *Music Forum* 1 (1967): 162–203.

32 Benjamin Boretz, "Meta-Variations" (Ph.D. diss., Princeton University, 1976), 435–501.

33 Ernst Kurth, *Romantische Harmonik und die Krise in Wagners Tristan* (Berlin: M. Hesse, 1923).

34 Ernst Kurth, *Grundlagen des linearen Kontrapunkts* (Berne: M. Drechsel, 1917).

35 Ernst Kurth, *Bruckner*, 2 vols. (Berlin: M. Hesse, 1925); idem, *Musikpsychologie* (Berlin: M. Hesse, 1931); idem, "Die Voraussetzungen der theoretischen Harmonik" (Habilitatimsschrift, University of Berne, 1912).

36 Heinrich Schenker, *Das Meisterwerk in der Musik* (Munich: Drei Masken Verlag, 1925), 1:93–96.

37 H. H. Stuckenschmidt, *Arnold Schoenberg* (London: John Calder, 1959), 52.

38 Paul Lansky, "Pitch-Class Consciousness," *Perspectives of New Music* 13/2 (1975): 30–56.

39 Milton Babbitt, "Since Schoenberg," *Perspectives of New Music* 12/1–2 (1973–74): 33.

6. The Unlikely Survival of Serious Music

1 Alban Berg, "Why is Schoenberg's Music So Difficult to Understand?" *Musikblatter des Anbruch*, September 1924; reprinted in Willi Reich, *Alban Berg*, trans. Cornelius Cardew (New York: Vienna House, 1974), 189–204.

2 Arnold Schoenberg, "Composition with Twelve Tones," in *Style and Idea*, ed. Leonard Stein, trans. Leo Black (Berkeley: University of California Press, 1984), 217.

3 William Mitchell.

4 *New York Times*, 19 January 1966.

5 Milton Babbitt, "Contemporary Music Composition and Music Theory as Contemporary Intellectual History," in *Perspectives in Musicology*, ed. B. Brook, E. Downes, and S. Van Solkema (New York: Norton, 1971), 151–84.

6 Daniel Bell, "The Disjunction of Culture and Social Structure: Some Notes on the Meaning of Social Reality," *Daedalus* (Winter, 1965): 220; reprinted in *Science and Culture*, ed. G. Holton (Boston: Houghton Mifflin, 1965).

7 Dwight Bolinger, *Aspects of Language* (New York: Harcourt Brace Jovanovich 1975), 31.

8 Ludwig Landgrebe, *Major Problems in Contemporary European Philosophy*, trans. K. Reinhardt (New York: Ungar, 1966). *Philosophie der Gegenwart* (Frankfurt: Ullsheim, 1957).

9 Walter Stace, *The Destiny of Western Man* (New York: Reynal and Hitchcock, 1942).

10 *Young Composers*, trans. Leo Black (Bryn Mawr, Pa.: Theodore Presser Co.; London: Universal Edition, 1960).

11 Nelson Goodman, "Credence, Credibility, Comprehension," *Journal of Philosophy* 76/11 (November 1979): 619.

Glossary

AGGREGATE   A collection containing all twelve pitch classes.

ALL-COMBINATORIALITY   The capacity of a collection to create aggregates with forms of itself and its complement under both transposition and inversion. Such a collection is all-combinatorial in that it possesses all four types of combinatoriality: prime-, inversional-, retrograde-, and retrograde-inversional-combinatoriality. Of the six all-combinatorial hexachords, three are "first-order" in that they can create aggregates at only one transposition level for each of the four traditional orderings of the series: prime, inversion, retrograde, and retrograde-inversion. Of the remaining three hexachords, one is "second-order" (creating aggregates at two levels), one is "third-order" (creating aggregates at three levels), and one is "sixth-order" (creating aggregates at six levels).

AREAS   Babbitt's use of the term "area" in twelve-tone music refers to a twelve-tone series and all transformations of it with the same hexachordal content. In the case of a series that is inversionally combinatorial at a single level (Schoenberg's typical kind of series), the usual forty-eight row forms can be grouped into twelve areas, each containing a row-form, the inversionally combinatorial row-form, and the retrogrades of each of these. As the number of combinatorial levels increases, the number of distinct areas decreases.

CIRCLE-OF-FOURTHS and CIRCLE-OF-FIFTHS TRANSFORM   The two most important multiplicative operations. The circle-of-fourths transform (M5) involves multiplying pitch-class integers by 5 (mod 12). M5 maps a chromatic scale onto a circle of fourths (and vice versa). The circle-of-fifths transform (M7) involves multiplying pitch-class integers by 7 (mod 12). M7 maps a chromatic scale onto a circle of fifths (and vice versa).

COLLECTION   An unordered group of pitch classes.

COMBINATORIALITY   The capacity of a collection to combine with some transformation of itself (or its complement) to form aggregates.

COMMUNALITY   The extent to which a group of compositions have structural elements in common. For example, the diatonic collection is an element of communality within the repertoire of much eighteenth- and nineteenth-century European music.

COMPLEMENT   For any collection, the pitch classes it excludes constitute its complement. The union of a collection and its complement is the aggregate. In reference to intervals, any two intervals which sum to an octave are called "complements mod 12."

CONTEXTUALITY   The extent to which a composition is self-referential, in that its structural elements are understood to be specific to the individual composition, rather than shared with other compositions.

DYAD   A collection of two pitch classes.

FIRST-ORDER   see ALL-COMBINATORIALITY.

HEXACHORD   A collection of six pitch classes.

INDEX NUMBER   For two inversionally-related collections or sets, the sum (mod 12) of any pitch class in one set or collection with the corresponding pitch class in the other set or collection is an index number. Given two sets or collections related by inversion, for any pitch-class x in the first there will be a corresponding pitch-class y in the second such that $x + y = n$. N is said to be their index number.

INTERVAL   An interval is the number of semitones between two pitches or pitch classes. Both pitch and pitch-class intervals may be either ordered or unordered. An ordered interval between two pitch classes is calculated by counting upward from the first pitch class to the second. There are eleven ordered pitch-class intervals (1, 2, 3, . . . 11). An unordered pitch-class interval (also called an interval class) is calculated by counting from the first pitch class to the second pitch class either upward or downward, whichever is shorter. There are six unordered pitch-class intervals (1, 2, 3, . . . 6).

INTERVAL MULTIPLICITY   The number of times a given interval class occurs between any pair of pitch classes in some collection.

INVERSION   An operation that maps one set or collection onto another by inverting each element around some axis and then transposing it by some interval. This
operation is abbreviated TnI (where I stands for inversion and Tn stands for
transposition by some interval n). Inversion is one of the four traditional twelve-
tone transformations.

INVERSIONAL COMBINATORIALITY   A collection is inversionally combinatorial (I-
combinatorial) if it can combine with an inversion of itself to create an aggregate.
A hexachord is I-combinatorial if its inversion at some transposition level is
equivalent to its complement.

INVERSIONAL SYMMETRY   A collection that maps onto itself under inversion is
inversionally symmetrical.

M5, M7   see CIRCLE-OF-FOURTHS and CIRCLE-OF-FIFTHS TRANSFORM.

MAPPING   Performing an operation on the elements of one object to transform it
into another is sometimes referred to as mapping the first object onto the second.

MOD 12   A system of arithmetic modulo 12. Two integers x and y are "equivalent
mod 12" if and only if $x = 12(n) + y$ for some integer n. In a mod 12 system, as
with the hours on a clockface, adding or subtracting 12 from some integer will
not change its identity.

PARTITIONING   The division of a collection or set into two or more exclusive
parts.

PERMUTATION   A change in ordering.

PITCH CLASS   A class of all pitches separated by one or more octaves. For example, all the individual pitches with the name A are members of pitch-class A. In
the well-tempered system, there are twelve pitch classes dividing the octave into
twelve equal parts. Pitch classes are normally represented by integers in one of two
ways. In "fixed *do*" notation, all C's (and B♯'s and D♭'s) are represented by 0, all
C♯'s and D♭'s by 1, all D's by 2, etc. In "moveable *do*" notation, 0 is assigned
to any convenient pitch class, often the first pitch class in the first statement of a
twelve-tone series, and the remaining pitch classes are assigned according to their
distance from that 0 measured in semitones.

PRIME COMBINATORIALITY   A collection is prime-combinatorial (P-combinatorial)
if it can combine with a transposition of itself to create an aggregate. A hexachord
is P-combinatorial if some transposition of it is equivalent to its complement.

RETROGRADE   An operation on order (usually of a twelve-tone series) in which the first element becomes the last element, the second element becomes the second-to-last, and so on. Retrograde is one of the traditional twelve-tone transformations.

RETROGRADE COMBINATORIALITY   A collection is retrograde-combinatorial (R-combinatorial) if it can combine with a transposition of its complement to create an aggregate. All hexachords are R-combinatorial in that they combine with their literal complement (transposed by 0 semitones) to create an aggregate. Some hexachords can also combine with their complement, transposed at levels other than 0.

RETROGRADE-INVERSION   An operation in which the series is inverted and then retrograded. Retrograde-inversion is one of the traditional twelve-tone transformations.

RETROGRADE-INVERSIONAL COMBINATORIALITY   A collection is retrograde-inversionally combinatorial (RI-combinatorial) if it can combine with an inversion of its complement to create an aggregate.

ROW   An ordering of the twelve pitch classes.

SECOND-ORDER   see ALL-COMBINATORIAL.

SELF-INVERSIONAL   The mapping of a collection onto itself under the operation of inversion.

SERIES   An ordering of the twelve pitch classes.

SET   An ordering of the twelve pitch classes. Some theorists use the term "set" for an unordered collection of pitch classes, but Babbitt uses it strictly as a synonym for "series."

SIMULTANEITY   A group of notes sounding simultaneously.

SIXTH-ORDER   see ALL-COMBINATORIAL.

TETRACHORD   A collection of four pitch classes.

THIRD-ORDER   see ALL-COMBINATORIAL.

"TO WITHIN"   An expression used to emphasize that an equivalence relationship is not an identity relationship. Thus two collections may be said to be equivalent "to within transposition" or "to within inversion," that is, the two collections are transpositions or inversions of one another. Similarly, two intervals which sum to an octave are equivalent "to within complementation," that is, are members of the same interval class.

TRANSPOSITION   An operation that maps one collection or set onto another by adding a fixed number (known as the "interval of transposition") to each pitch class of the first collection or set. This operation is abbreviated Tn (where T stands for transposition and n for the interval of transposition).

TRICHORD   A collection of three pitch classes.

TWELVE-BY-TWELVE   A matrix in which each row and column is one of the forty-eight forms of a twelve-tone series. Prime forms are read from left to right; retrogrades from right to left; inversions from top to bottom; and retrograde-inversions from bottom to top.

-TYPE   (as in trichord-type, tetrachord-type, etc.) Two collections are members of the same collection-type if they are related to each other by transposition or inversion.

Index

Aggregate, 44, 51, 68, 90–91, 92; weighted (partial) 100–101 (Ex. 4-15). *See also* Schoenberg; Webern

Albrechtsberger, Johann Georg, 124

All-combinatorial hexachords, 54, 93, 97–98; and all-interval sets, 51–52; first order (♯1, ♯2, ♯3), 46, 48–49 (Ex. 2-16), 50–51 (Ex. 2-17), 52 , 53 (Ex. 2-19), 86, 93–94 (Exs. 4-6, 4-7), 96–97 (Exs. 4-12, 4-13); hexachordal areas (regions), 52, 53–54 (Ex. 2-18), 94–96 (Exs. 4:7–11); hierarchical relationships among, 48–51 (Exs. 2-16, 2-17), 54–55 (Ex. 2-19); second order (♯4), 52–53 (Ex. 2-18a), 54–55 (Ex. 2-19), 108, 114 (Ex. 4-27), 114–16 (Exs. 4-28, 4-29), 116–17; third order (♯5), 52, 53 (Ex. 2-18b), 114 (Ex. 4-27), 117; trichordal generation of, 46, 48, 50–51 (Ex. 2-17), 54 (Ex. 2-19), 86–87 (Exs. 4-1, 4-2), 88–90 (Exs. 4-4, 4-5), 91–92, 93, 94–97 (Exs. 4:7–13); whole tone (♯6), 53–54 (Ex. 2-18c)

All-combinatorial tetrachords, 77–78, 120 (Ex. 4-32). *See also* Tetrachords

All-interval twelve-tone set, 51–52, 107

All-trichordal twelve-tone set, 106–7 (Exs. 4-18, 4-19)

Ansonia Hotel, 7

"Applied dominants," 134

Array of partitions, 98–99 (Ex. 4-14); inversion of entire array, 102–4 (Exs. 4-16, 4-17); inversion of paired lines to create weighted aggregates, 99–101 (Ex. 4-15)

Artin, Emil, 104

Aspects of Language. See Bolinger, Dwight

Association: in array of partitions, 99; in *Moses and Aaron*, 82–84 (Exs. 3-16, 3-17); in Schoenberg's *Orchestra Piece* Op. 16, No. 1, 158 (Ex. 5-24)

Associative harmony, 146, 148–50 (Exs. 5-16, 5-17), 161–62 (Exs. 5-29, 5-30)

Audience: for twentieth-century music, 174

Austin, John, 182

Babbitt, Milton: early activities of, 5, 6–7, 30–32; and generalizations of techniques of Schoenberg and Webern, 24–25; influence of series in music of, 27–28 (Exs. 1-14, 1-15), 29–30 (Exs. 1-17, 1-18); influences upon, 24, 24–25; "maximum variety" in twelve-tone structure, 87–88 (Ex. 4-3); as music theorist, 122; and proof of hexachordal theorem, 104–6

Musical Works and Writings: *All Set* 116–17; *Ars Combinatoria*, 107 (Ex. 4-19); *Composition for Four Instruments*, 26, 27–28 (Exs. 1-14, 1-15); "Contemporary Music Composition and Music Theory as Contemporary Intellectual History," 190; *Du*, 26; *Images*, 106 (Ex. 4-18); *Minute Waltz*, 26; *Music for the Mass*, 32; "The Music Theoretician's Dilemmas," 188; *Partitions*, 89, 97; *Post-Partitions*, 89; *Reflections for Piano and Tape*, 93, 100; "Since Schoenberg," 51, 161, 188, 190; "Some Aspects of Twelve-Tone Composition," 187; "Stravinsky's Verticals and (Schoenberg's) Diagonals: A Twist of Fate," 188; *String Quartet No. 2*, 28–30 (Exs. 1:16–18), 93, 100; *Three Compositions for Piano*, 26

Bach, C. P. E., 127, 170

Bach, J. S., 8, 127, 156, 170

Musical Works: Cantata BWV 153, 125; Chorale ♯117, 137–43 (Ex. 5-13); Chorale ♯217, 124–25, 125–27 (Ex. 5-1), 128–33 (5:2–8); chorales, 131–32, 152; *Partita in E Major* (for solo violin), 156

Barnard College, 19

Bartók, Béla, 51, 178–79

"Basic set," 12

Bauer, Marion, 7; *Twentieth-Century Music:*

Dominant, "applied." *See* "Applied dominants"
Double leading-tone technique, 153–54 (Ex. 5-20)
Der Dreiklang: Monatsschrift für Musik, 144, 189
Duffy, Edward: *Four Analyses of the Prelude to Tristan: A Review*, 190
Dvořák, Antonín: Cello Concerto, 141–42
Dylan, Bob, 181

Electronic (and computer) music, 172–74, 176
Eliot, T. S., 173
Engel, Lehman, 5, 187
Erpf, Hermann, 18, 134–36 (Exs. 5:9–11), 143, 153–54 (Ex. 5-20); *Studien zur Harmonie und Klangtechnik der Neueren Musik*, 134, 189
Explanation, sufficient. *See* Discourse, musical

Faulkner, William, 181
58th Street Library, 6
Figured-bass numbers, 20
"Form," 72
Forte, Allen, 121
Fox, Ralph, 105–6
"Fragmentation of musical activity" ("pluralism"), 164, 165–66, 168–69, 172
French Conservatory, 152
French Opera, 152
"Fresh" note notion, 155
Furtwängler, Wilhelm, 148, 149
Fux, J. J., 17, 124

Goethe, Johann W. von, 119–20
Goodman, Nelson, 182, 191

Hammett, Dashiell, 181
Hannenheim, Norbert von, 10, 187
Harmony: "functional" ("Rameau-based"), 127–28 (Ex. 5-2), 133–34, 136, 138–39, 141, 145; governed by relations internal to a piece, 89, 139, 142–43; teaching of, 125–26 (Ex. 5-1), 127, 131–32 (Ex. 5-7), 132–33 (Ex. 5-8), 138–39; in Webern's *Symphony*, Op. 21, 45. *See also* Associative harmony; Chorale harmonization
Harvard University, 6, 177
Hexachord(s): in Babbitt's Second String Quartet, 29–30 (Exs. 1-17, 1-18); construction of Schoenbergian, 55–57 (Ex. 2-20); intervallic content of complementary, 15 (Ex. 1-5), 104–5; from *Jakobsleiter* (self-inversional), 13–16 (Exs. 1-4, 1-5), 46–47 (Exs. 2-14, 2-15), 57–58 (Ex. 2-21); relations between trichords and, 24–26 (Exs. 1-12, 1-13), 30 (Ex. 1-18), 45–46 (Ex. 2-13), 46, 48, 50–51 (Ex. 2-17), 54–55 (Ex. 2-19), 85–87 (Exs. 4-1, 4-2), 88–90 (Exs. 4-4, 4-5), 92, 93, 93–97 (Exs. 4:6–13); of Schoenberg's Fourth Quartet, 37 (Ex. 1-7), 21–22 (Exs. 1-8a, b), 23 (Ex. 1-11), 65–67 (Exs. 3:2–4); of Stravinsky's *Movements*, 108 (Exs. 4-20, 4-21),

111–12 (Exs. 4-24, 4-25), 112–13, 114 (Ex. 4-27); structural influence of, 29–30 (Exs. 1-17, 1-18), 44–45, 91–92; in Webern's *Symphony*, Op. 21, 42–43 (Ex. 2-10), 44–45. *See also* All-combinatorial hexachords; Hexachordal combinatoriality
Hexachordal areas, 52, 94–96 (Exs. 4:7–11)
Hexachordal combinatoriality: inversional (Schoenbergian), 14–15 (Exs. 1-4, 1-5), 20–21, 23 (Ex. 1-11), 46–47 (Ex. 2-14), 52, 55–57 (Ex. 2-20), 68, 75, 85, 93 (Ex. 4-6). *See also* All-combinatorial hexachords
Hexachordal theorem, 15, 104, 104–6
Hierarchization: in late Stravinsky, 107; in twelve-tone music, 19 (Ex. 1-7), 20–21, 34, 68, 107, 118, 171. *See also* All-combinatorial hexachords
High Fidelity, 122–23, 188
Hindemith, Paul, 32, 155; String Quartet #3, 154–55 (Ex. 5-21), 160

Index number, 34, 51, 60–61 (Exs. 2:24–26), 100–101, 102–3 (Ex. 4-16), 103–4 (Ex. 4-17), 162; and construction of combinatorial hexachords, 55–58 (Exs. 2-20, 2-21); in Dallapiccola, 39–40 (Exs. 2-6, 2-7); in Webern, 34–35, 37–38
Indiana University, 107
Inference of structural properties from musical surface, 117–18
Institute for Advanced Studies, 123–24
Intuition, 104, 106–7 (Exs. 4-18, 4-19)
Inversion: array of partitions and, 99–104 (Exs. 4:14–17); of contour, 75; dyadic invariance between paired, inversionally-related twelve-tone sets, 33–35 (Exs. 2-1, 2-2), 36–37 (Exs. 2-3, 2-4), 37–38, 38–40 (Exs. 2:5–7); extension of property of "dyadic invariance between paired, inversionally-related twelve-tone sets," 40–42 (Exs. 2-8, 2-9); of order. *See* Order inversion
Inversional canon. *See* Canon, inversional
Inversional combinatoriality. *See* Hexachordal combinatoriality

Jackson, Mississippi, 5
Jadassohn, Salomon, 146, 147, 190; *Melodik und Harmonik bei Richard Wagner*, 190
Jonas, Oswald: "Mozart's ewigen Melodie," *Der Dreiklang: Monatsschrift für Musik*, 189
Joyce, James, 81
Juilliard, 177; job offer to Schoenberg, 7
Juilliard Quartet, 178

Kaminski, Heinrich, 155
Kassler, Michael, 90
Kette, 153
Kirnberger, J. P., 17, 127; *Die Kunst des reinen Satzes in der Musik*, 189
Kohl, Jerome, 114; "Exposition in Stravinsky's Orchestral *Variations*," 188
Krenek, Ernst, 6, 10, 27, 155

Kurth, Ernst, 155–56; *Grundlagen des linearen Kontrapunkts*, 155, 190; *Die Voraussetzungen der theoretischen Harmonik*, 155, 190; other writings of, 190

Landgrebe, Ludwig: *Philosophie der Gegenwart*, 181–82, 191
Language: analogy with music, 9–10, 171–72
Lansky, Paul, 161, 190; "Pitch-Class Consciousness," 190
Leibnitz, Gottfried W., 122
Leipzig Conservatory, 146
Lennon, John, 181
Lewin, David, 104–6
Linear counterpoint, 155
Liquidation technique, 19
Liszt, Franz: *Eine Faust Symphonie*, 136 (Ex. 5-11), 153, 162
Locke, John, 122
Lorenz, Alfred, 148–49, 155, 190; *Das Geheimnis der Form bei Richard Wagner*, 190
"The Lyceum of Schoenberg." *See* Weiss, Adolph

M5 transform. *See* Circle-of-fifths transformation
Major Problems in Contemporary European Philosophy, 182
Mancini, Henry, 181
Mannes School, 143
Marpurg, F. W., 127
Mattheson, Johann: *Der volkommene Capellmeister*, 145, 189
"Maximum variety" in twelve-tone structure, 87–88 (Ex. 4-3)
Melancholy Baby, 18, 148
Memory, musical, 145
The Merry Widow, 140
Metrical projection of twelve-tone sets, 43–44 (Exs. 2-11, 2-12)
"Middle period" music (of Schoenberg, Webern, Berg), 8, 9–10, 140, 167–68, 170
"Minimum mutilation," 49, 170
Mitchell, William, 156, 189, 190; *Elementary Harmony*, 125, 189; "The *Tristan* Prelude: Techniques and Structure," 155, 190
Mizler, Lorenz, 141
Modulation, 18
Motive, 171. *See also* Schoenberg, Arnold: "composing with the tones of a motive"
Mozart, W. A., 32, 71, 170; Clarinet Quintet, mvmt. 3, 143–44 (Ex. 5-14), 147; as teacher, 145–46
Multifunctionality of a pitch class, 90–91, 92–93
Multiplicative transform. *See* Circle-of-fifths transformation
Music, twentieth-century; audience for, 174; crisis of, 172; as different from earlier music, 165; difficulties, 166–68, 168–69, 170, 171–72; electronic (and computer), 172–74, 176. *See also* Twelve-tone music; Comprehensibility and twentieth-century music
Music Forum, 122
Musical Leader, 5, 187
Musical Quarterly, 147
Music theory (theorists): influence of, 122, 123, 124; professional, 121–22; and Schenker, 175
Music Theory Spectrum, 122, 147

Nabokov, Nicholas, 125–26
New York City, 5, 177, 182
New York Times, 190
New York University (Washington Square College), 6, 7
Nordoff, Paul, 31, 188

On Wisconsin, 31
Order inversion, 111, 118–19
Ordering and collection, relationship between, 20–21, 26, 68, 107
Oster, Ernst, 134, 151–52, 189
Overtone series, 122

Parallelism(s): in Bach chorales, 128–29 (Exs. 5-3, 5-4), 131–33 (Exs. 5-7, 5-8), 138 (Ex. 5-13), 139, 140–41; in functions of a single pitch class, 90–91, 92–93; in Mozart's Clarinet Quintet, mvmt. 2, 144; Mozart's teaching of, 145–46; in Wagner, 147, 148–49
Partial aggregate. *See* Aggregate, weighted
Partitioning, general, 97–99 (Ex. 4-14)
Partition notation, 99
"Paths through a piece." *See* Chains of relationships
Perception of music: and conceptualization, 23, 24, 44, 64, 72; and new boundary conditions, 172–73; "sweet and sour" beats, 144. *See also* Memory, musical
Performance: determination of what is performed, 123; influence of analysis on, 143–44 (Ex. 5-14), 144
Perkins, John: "Dallapiccola's Art of Canon," 38, 188
Perle, George, 105
Perspectives of New Music, 114
Philadelphia, 31
"Phrases," 138
Piston, Walter: *Harmony*, 130, 189
Pitch class, 22 (Ex. 1-9); numerical notation of, 19–20
Popper, Karl, 182
"Pre-compositional," 90
Princeton University, 32, 124, 125, 177, 182
Projection of twelve-tone sets. *See* Twelve-tone set: projection of
Proust, Marcel, 181
Prussian Academy, 10
Purcell, Henry: "Brief Introduction to the Art of Descant," 145, 189

Quine, W. V. O., 182

DESIGNED BY DAVID FORD
COMPOSED BY IMPRESSIONS, INC., MADISON, WISCONSIN
MANUFACTURED BY THOMSON-SHORE, INC., DEXTER, MICHIGAN
TEXT AND DISPLAY LINES ARE SET IN SABON

Library of Congress Cataloging-in-Publication Data
Babbitt, Milton, 1916–
   Milton Babbitt: words about music.
      (The Madison Lectures)
Includes bibliographical references and index.
1. Music—20th century—History and criticism.
I. Dembski, Stephen. II. Straus, Joseph Nathan.
   III. Title. IV. Title: Words about music.
               V. Series.
ML60.B125   1986   780'.904   86-40455
            ISBN 0-299-10790-6